Praise for *Destiny vs. Choice*

"For those seeking clarity…take heart. *Destiny vs. Choice* is the consummate intellectual toolkit you've been waiting for! Jones has done the homework for you, but in the final analysis, it is your choice."
—Marshall Masters, *Crossing the Cusp* and host of Cut to the Chase Radio

"Free will or fate…do you know? Marie Jones takes on one of the biggest mysteries that human beings face in her new book *Destiny vs. Choice*. Religion, tarot cards, evolution, karma, soul mate and many other topics are discussed in the book that will leave you wondering in awe at the great mystery of life."
—Sandy Andrew, The Universal Learning Series Radio Show

"With a characteristic witty twist of pen and her trademark plethora of researched information, Marie D. Jones magically untangles this universal question in clear, enlightening and empowering ways for all."
—Astrid Stromberg, host of Brilliant Essence Radio, international psychic, clinical hypnotherapist and Reiki master

Destiny vs. Choice

The Scientific and Spiritual Evidence Behind Fate and Free Will

Marie D. Jones

New Page BOOKS

Pompton Plains, NJ

DESTINY VS. CHOICE
EDITED BY JODI BRANDON
TYPESET BY GINA TALUCCI

Image on page 18 courtesy of Wikimedia Commons; Image on page 52 courtesy of Japa-nese-symbols.org; Image on page 52 courtesy of chinesenames.org; Images on pages 55, 64, 73, 109 courtesy of Wikipedia; Image on page 68 courtesy of Dark Sun Studios; Image on page 76 courtesy of Bev Walton-Porter; Image on page 80 courtesy of Cheryl Deist; Image on page 191 courtesy of Rich Vossler; Image on page 205 courtesy of Eric Rankin; image on page 208 courtesy of Sally Richards; Image on page 214 courtesy of Marie D. Jones

Cover design by Ian Shimkoviak/the BookDesigners
Printed in the U.S.A.

To order this title, please call toll-free 1-800-CAREER-1 (NJ and Canada: 201-848-0310) to order using VISA or MasterCard, or for further information on books from Career Press.

The Career Press, Inc.
220 West Parkway, Unit 12
Pompton Plains, NJ 07444
www.careerpress.com
www.newpagebooks.com

Library of Congress Cataloging-in-Publication Data

Jones, Marie D., 1961-
    Destiny vs. choice : the scientific and spiritual evidence behind fate and free will / by Marie D. Jones.
        p. cm.
    Includes bibliographical (p.   ) references and index.
    ISBN 978-1-60163-156-5 -- ISBN 978-1-60163-670-6 (ebook) 1. Fate and fatalism. 2. Free will and determinism. I. Title. II.
    Title: Destiny versus choice.

BJ1461.J66 2011
123--dc22
                                                                    2011010738

Dedicated to Max,
who is MY destiny.

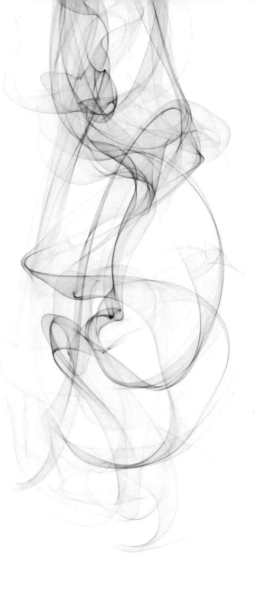

Acknowledgments

I would like to thank the usual suspects in my life who take on the roles of friends, cheerleaders, and supporters. That would be my mom, Milly Savino, and my dad, John Savino, who never cease to believe in me and love me whether I am brilliant or a bonehead, and often I am both... even at the same time! Thank you to my sister and best pal, Angella Gonzalez, and my beloved bro, John Savino, and all the extended family that provide me with so much love and laughter. Winnie, Alana, Aaron, Efren, Ally, Sadie, Sugar, Chow, Lucy, and all the rest, I love you for being part of my daily life.

Thank you to all of my friends and colleagues throughout the years, way too numerous to mention, but big thanks to Helen Cooper (onward and upward!) and Andrea Glass for their ongoing support. Thank you Aaron White for taking such good care of my web presence. Thank you to Bruce Lucas for helping me realize big dreams. Thanks Ron Jones, for all your help and friendship. And thanks to Larry Flaxman for being my co-author, business partner, and dear friend.

To all those who have "friended" me and "followed" me on Facebook and Twitter and LinkedIn, come to see me speak, listened to me on the radio, or purchased and actually read my books—I cannot even thank you enough. Without all of you, I'd be preaching to the wall! Really, you are all so wonderful to me.

Thank you to my agent, Lisa Hagan, who I am proud to say is also my good friend. To everyone at New Page Books—Michael, Laurie, and the entire staff—and the folks at Warwick Associates—Simon, Kate, Maggie, and Amanda—for allowing me to do what I do and get the work out into the world, a heartfelt thanks for everything.

But most of all, thank you to the one who makes my destiny the most special destiny of all: my brilliant, hilarious, and adorable son, Max, without whom the path of my life would not be worth traveling.

Contents

Introduction

"You can't avoid it, it's written in the stars."
"We were meant to be."
"He was destined to be a success."
"She chose to be a failure."
"Life is what you make it."
"Choose your thoughts and choose your life."

Throughout our lives, we are bombarded with contradictory claims that our lives are predestined, that Fate deals us the cards we will play our entire lives with, that whatever happens, happens for a reason, *or* that our lives are what we choose them to be, that what we focus on expands and manifests, that it's all just one big crapshoot. Confused, many of us don't know if there is indeed a blueprint for our lives laid down before we are born, or we are entirely on our own and left to our own defenses—making it up as we go along.

Destiny vs. Choice promises to explore both sides of the fence, examining both scientific and spiritual evidence to support either argument. From the concepts of pre-ordainment, past lives, and the Book of Life to the law of attraction, the power of intention, and the role of the observer in perceiving reality, this book will cover the most cutting-edge science, philosophy, religious, and metaphysical theories and beliefs pertaining to the battle between destiny and choice. It will also include many personal stories written by people who have experienced one, the other—or a blend of both, for maybe our lives are a combination of the two.

This book hopes to open up the discussion and move toward answers to the following questions:

··· If our lives are predestined, what role do we have, if any, in where we end up, with whom, and doing what?

··· If it's all up to us, how do we ever know if we are living the right life, on the right track, or truly following our path?

··· Are we all just playing out roles that were chosen for us prior to our birth? Or are we choosing the roles we play as we go along?

··· What are the links between destiny and quantum physics? Between quantum physics and free will?

··· How do evolution and intelligent design relate to destiny and choice?

··· Is it all really written in the stars? Can astrology and numerology really reveal our life paths?

··· How does DNA fit into the argument of human destiny versus individual choice and free will? If we are individually molded physically before birth, are we also molded consciously? Could our DNA also contain our spiritual destiny?

··· What are the roles of synchronicity and intuition in destiny and in free will?

··· How does the law of attraction work with both destiny and free will?

··· What do stories of ghosts and life after death have to tell us about destiny and about individual choice?

··· What do the world's religions and philosophical systems say about destiny and free will?

··· What role does suffering play in destiny and in choice?

··· Is there a collective destiny, and a collective free will, that makes up shared reality? How do our choices and paths affect others, and how do theirs affect us?

··· How can we use our destiny and our own free will to empower our lives and bring us more love, joy, and success?

Destiny vs. Choice is a philosophical battle that may not end any time soon, because evidence for one, the other, and both keeps showing up in the course of our lives. But maybe, just maybe, this book will serve to show how perhaps the truth lies somewhere in between and, how no matter what you believe, your life is a reflection of that belief.

Destiny...Fate *or* free will...choice? Which path will you choose to take?

> "A consistent soul believes in destiny,
> a capricious one in chance."
> —Benjamin Disraeli

One

The Battle of the Ages

"It's choice, not chance, that determines your destiny."
—Jean Nidetch

"It is in your moments of decision that your destiny is shaped."
—Anthony Robbins

"I have noticed even people who claim everything is predestined, and that we can do nothing to change it, look before they cross the road."
—Stephen Hawking

What is a life, but a collection of choices leading to a freely chosen end? What is a life but a predetermined path that, like it or not, one must follow or pay the price of eternal unhappiness? What is a life but—oh, forget it. We could do this all day. The battle over destiny and free will, fate and choice, "set in stone" and "just wing it, baby" has been going on forever, perhaps even since the moment humans emerged from the murk of evolutionary destiny. Or would that be evolutionary free will?

Is a life nothing but choices made, that build upon each other to create either a life well lived, a life barely lived, or a life tolerated? Or is life something we come fully prepared into, with all the tools, ammunition, and gear we need to end up exactly where we need to be, with whom we need to be there, and when we need to be there?

To understand the argument itself, we first need to know what destiny and free will really are. We may think of them as simple concepts, but, as humans are often wont to do, they end up far more complex and sophisticated. In fact, there isn't just one kind of destiny, or one kind of free will. No, we have to muddle up the debate with tangents and bullet points, offshoots and exemptions and all kinds of factors that go way beyond the simplicity of "my life is predestined" and "my life is my choices combined."

So let's start unraveling the complexity of it all. We will start with destiny.

Destiny in Its Many Forms

Fate. Fortune. Kismet. Serendipity. The Master Plan. We all at some point feel a sense of destiny about something we experience in life. Whether a romantic coupling, an incredible career change, or that perfect new home, things sometimes fall into place as if someone "up there" is working a gigantic jigsaw puzzle that is our life.

Destiny means a predetermined course of events often held to be an irresistible power or agency. It comes from the Middle English "destinee," and the Anglo-French "destineé." The first known use of the word comes from the 14th century, but most likely the concept has been around since humankind first began to contemplate its individual and collective naval.

Destiny is one's lot in life. One's circumstances. The cards one was dealt and now must play. But destiny is not necessarily the same as fate.

In Greek and Roman mythology, three goddesses are responsible for the dispensation of fate. The Greeks had their "Moirae" and the Romans had "Parcae." Even the Norse had three "Norns." For some reason, three goddesses were required to dole out the events and circumstances one was fated to experience. What differentiates destiny and fate is the total lack of free choice that is found in fate. Fate implies such a fixed outcome, always ending in the "fatality" of death, that choice has little room to exist.

Destiny, on the other hand, can include healthy doses of choice and free will, but always ends with the determined, or predetermined result.

The Greek goddess Tyche represented good fortune. Her Roman counterpart was Fortuna, and she turned the mighty wheel of fortune long before Pat Sajak and Vanna White ever existed. Good fortune, though, is more associated with chance and luck, which we will discuss in a later chapter. Fate, on the other hand, was not about luck. Because...if you were fated to be decapitated at the hands of Roman soldiers, sadly there was no wiggle room for any last-minute strokes of luck. Fate and fatalism are sold "as is."

The presence of such goddesses is proof that some sense of feeling that life is planned out in advance has always been a part of the dialog of humanity. And of course, religious texts are abundant with references to who was destined to do what, as if the finger of God touched certain men and women, some with greatness, others

Fig. 1

The Greek Moirae were three goddesses who dispensed fate.
Their names were Clotho, Lachesis, and Atropos.

with the burden of unimaginable suffering. You had no choice. If God chose you to save the world, you accepted that destiny and ran with it. As did Christ. If God wanted you to be eaten by a whale and learn your lessons, you accepted your destiny and, well, sat there and contemplated your lot. As did Jonah.

The idea that we all have a bullet with our name on it, or that there is a specific, preordained time for our number to come up, often leads to the belief that certain groups of people are "chosen" over others. This is one of the negative aspects of destiny, that one race should be touched by the hand of God and others rejected, but this was the driving force for the entire idea of America's "Manifest Destiny" that proclaimed in the 1850s the superiority of America and its role in shaping the world. This may have originated in an earlier idea of the New World of the Puritans as the "New Jerusalem" that the chosen ones were destined to find and establish. What better place than a land filled with possibilities—well, at least once you got rid of all those pesky natives. Then, destiny was yours to rise to, to aspire to.

We can even have a love of destiny itself, an *amor fati*, or love of fate. The term was coined by 19th-century German philosopher Friedrich Nietzsche, who described it as a belief that whatever happened to a person was good, including suffering and loss, because it is all a part of the path to destiny. *Amor fati* implies accepting anything and everything that happens to you as being just the way it is supposed to be. He wrote in his book *The Gay Science* of *amor fati* as allowing him to see the beauty in all things: "Amor fati: let that be my love henceforth! I do not want to wage war against what is ugly. I do not want to accuse; I do not even want to accuse those who accuse. Looking away shall be my only negation...."

This attitude of full and complete acceptance was, to Nietzsche, a way for a person to want nothing in life to be different than it was, and to bear what is necessary in life, even to love it—the good, the bad and the ugly. This may seem a bit extreme and remove all aspects of personal control, action, and will, and for a man who many argue was atheist, a bit in the direction of a higher power or directive overseeing one's life, with we, the little humans, only to accept it all and love it as is. Yet one of his prevailing philosophies, the honest questioning of all beliefs and doctrines that drain one of life force and energy, which he called "life-affirmation," works quite well with the concept of complete acceptance and surrender to what *is* instead of the suffering that occurs when we ache and strain and strive for what *is not*.

Predestination usually has religious undertones, because there is always the presence of some divine source that determines the course of a person, a nation, a world. Where the pagan cultures associated this source with various gods and goddesses, the Western world associated it with God. But one did not need to be religious to believe in some sort of destiny.

The world of philosophy probably wins the contest hands down when it comes to the argument pro and con. Whether we are talking about causality, determinism, fatalism, synchronicity, or plain old "lot in life," the philosophical angle was most responsible for taking a simplistic concept and giving it many variations from which to, ahem, choose. For now, we will attempt to leave religion out of it as much as possible, if only because that is discussed at length in the next chapter.

Determinism

Determinism, or "causal" determinism, is the belief that everything that happens to us is predictable—has a cause, so to speak, according to previous events. Thus, what happens to us in terms of actions, behaviors, and experiences is based upon what happened just before that, and just before that, and so on, and so on. Causal law rules the universe according to the philosophy of determinism, in a chain of events that lead from A to Z in a recognizable and rational manner.

God is not a necessity here, as in predestination. Determinism is all about cause and effect, and no God is required to keep that infinite chain of events moving along like falling dominoes, each one knocking down the next one in front of it. Nothing is "not caused" or caused by self here, taking out the element of pure free will. Whereas self-determination is all about choices one makes that lead to other choices, true determinism takes self out of the picture entirely. Humans are not free to use their will in true determinism. It's all preset and in motion as effects following the causes before them, like a fine-tuned machine.

Determining Determinism

There are different types of determinism, because philosophers, if nothing else, like to break ideas down into the smallest possible denominators, so here are a few:

- **Logical determinism:** All propositions about past, present, and future are either true or false. Future events, because already fixed, take away free will/choice.

- **Psychological determinism:** Human beings act according to reason and their own best interest.

- **Theological determinism:** God determines in advance everything that humans will do, think, act upon, become. Again, little or no free will leg-room here.

- **Historical determinism:** Various forces determine the historical and political course of events, related to the Marxist concept of dialectical materialism.

- **Technological determinism:** Reductionist theory stating that technology drives the social structure and cultural makeup of a society.

- **Biological determinism:** Our behaviors, desires, and actions are all genetic in nature.

- **Behavioral determinism:** All actions and events are reactions to our environmental conditioning.

··· **Cultural determinism:** *Same as behavioral determinism, but substitute cultural for environmental.*

··· **Environmental determinism:** *Our geographical location and physical environment determine our actions and responses.*

Fatalism

Fatalism is perhaps the most recognized form of determinism. A fatalist believes that all events are predetermined. It's all left up to Fate. There is no room whatsoever for true free will because it does not exist. Other tenets of fatalism include the belief that actions may be of our free will, but they still move us toward a predetermined end point. In terms of the collective destiny, we are all fated to move toward one path of history, and that path is our Fate. No matter how many "choices" we make within that context, we still must understand, according to fatalism, that we will end up in the same place.

Fatalism has similarities to the ideas of compatibilism and incompatibilism. When it comes to destiny and choice, there are so many categories and sub-categories people might get so confused, they give up and just "let go and go with the flow!" Compatibalism allows free will and determinism to be compatible, but only by allowing choice and will to be a link in the already-determined causal chain of events. So, you are using your free will to make a choice, but that choice is nothing more than an already-linked link in the cause and effect chain. Another name for this concept is "soft determinism," simply because it allows for a little bit of wiggle room for free will. Unlike pure fatalism, here you can at least think you have a choice, even if that choice still gets you to the same end result. ("Que sera, sera…whatever will be, will be, the future's not ours to see" goes an old song….)

Compatibilism allows man free will but that free will must be a link in the chain of causality. Aristotle put a twist on this, though, with what he called "*archai*," or fresh starting points that created new causal chains not related to or predictable from previous events. Thus it is possible to have causality without determinism when we deal with an uncaused event that starts a whole new chain.

Chance and Compatibility

Incompatibilism, on the other hand, states that for free will to exist, there must be an admittance of indeterminism. If determinism is the truth, then free will is incompatible with it. Free will is nothing but an illusion in the realm of determinism. But if you can prove that determinism is not the reality, then free will can exist. A key philosopher, Robert Kane, who is the editor of the *Oxford Handbook of Free Will*, admits that the problem of free will is an ongoing one, and he has spent decades trying to find a way to explain free will within indeterminism. Others, such as William James, in *Hard Determinism*, just simply call free will an illusion and that it is mutually exclusive from determinism. Indeterminism, thus, is the event that occurs without a cause, as in a chance event like the flip of a coin or the turn of a card. The result of the coin toss or card turn would be a probability until the event occurred, rather than a cause. The end result of heads or tales is nothing more than the chance outcome of the flip or toss and was not a predictable, or predetermined, event.

Chance, from the Latin *cadere*, or "to fall," allows for probability and unpredictability of the future. We can have a very different future if heads is the end result of the coin toss, rather than tails. This speaks a little to the idea of quantum uncertainty, which will be discussed in a later chapter. Suffice it to say, the idea that at the quantum level nothing is certain and all is probability does not bode well for a belief in determinism, or predestination.

Epicurus, ancient Greek philosopher and founder of the Epicurean philosophy, was perhaps the first philosopher to give a potential physical explanation for chance. Influenced by the teachings of

Aristotle, he believed that all events in the Universe were the result of the motions and interactions of atoms moving in empty space. Similar to the principles of fellow atomist Democritus, his belief centered on the idea that indivisible bits of matter (atoms, from the Greek *atomos*, "indivisible") flying through empty space (*khaos*) were responsible for everything that occurs. When these atoms are colliding, rebounding, and becoming entangled with one another, there is no predetermined plan behind their motions. The atoms don't always follow in straight lines, but may on occasion swerve or waver, allowing for a more quantum-like motion of fundamental particles. This allows for a bit of free will amidst a bit of determinism, something that many of Epicurus's contemporaries argued valiantly against.

Chances Are...

Chance confuses even the greatest of thinkers. Many philosophers simply deny that chance can exist, because it is pure nonsense to think that a current event is totally independent of any events that came before it. According to James Hastings's *Encyclopedia of religion and Ethics* (Part 10), Chrysippus, a Stoic philosopher, said around 200 BC, "Everything that happens is followed by something else which depends on it by causal necessity." He suggested that everything has to have a cause, and that if any uncaused movement is introduced into the system, the system would collapse and disintegrate.

Mathematical theorist Pierre-Simon Laplace says of chance in *A Philosophical Essay on Probabilities*, "The word 'chance' then expresses only our ignorance of the causes of the phenomena that we observe to occur and to succeed one another in no apparent order."

Earlier experiments involving chance showed that there indeed is a normal distribution of outcomes for ideal random processes, say the toss of a coin or throw of dice, which suggests that the phenomena of chance is really determined, and not random at all.

What are the chances of that?
This text was adapted from www.informationphilospher.com.

In his book *How Free Are You?* Ted Honderich states about determinism, "Determinism is the theory that our choices and decisions and what gives rise to them are effects." Thus, the chain of cause and effects is what leads to more causes and more effects, determining the final outcome of an event, or a life.

These theories totally leave out the potential of anything non-material in existence, such as a human soul that may have some influence on the actions and behaviors of a human being. Unless, of course, the soul is part of that deterministic structure, the chain linked fence of cause and effect, or, the soul exists but does not exert any causal influence upon exterior events.

It gets utterly nitpicky down here in philosophical hell, trying to pin down whether or not we are nothing but robots moving along a track like cars at an amusement park, or drivers on the Autobahn with the choices of going where they want as fast as they want, or something in between. The greatest minds that ever walked the earth have struggled with this argument, including the likes of Marcus Aurelius, Immanuel Kant, Baruch Spinoza, William James, Albert Einstein, Karl Marx, David Bohm, Neils Bohr, Friedrich Nietzsche, John Searle, and B.F. Skinner. Not to mention the religious masters who wrestled with the concepts and how they related to the presence, or non-presence, of a God figure.

First Cause

Take the idea of cause and effect. What is "First Cause"? According to deism, our universe has been here since the moment of creation, and has been deterministic in nature since that time. But, what was the First Cause that actually started the process of existence? Was it a choice made by a God? Some totally random event that simply triggered the resulting domino chain of causes and effects? If we understand that all causes have a prior event, what was the first "prior event?"

Did God start the process but, as deism teaches, have nothing to do with the chain of events that followed? Why on earth, no pun intended, would God start something He/She had no intention of finishing, or at least playing an ongoing role in? This is a basic "hole" in the 17th-century idea of deism. It makes little sense, even if it does conveniently provide a First Cause.

Marcus Aurelius Antoninus, Roman Emperor from A.D. 161 to 180, was a Stoic philosopher committed to a fatalistic atomistic theory. He had a slave named Epictetus, who was also a famous Stoic. One day Epictetus broke an expensive vase and the Emperor began beating him. Epictetus turned to his master and asked: "Why do you beat me? Is it by the philosophy we both believe in that it was predetermined from all time that I should break this vase?" Marcus Aurelius allegedly answered by saying, "By that same philosophy, it was predetermined from the beginning of all time that I should beat you" and continued beating his slave. This may sound more like the perfect excuse for any kind of abuse, and it is, if both parties buy into the concept of fatalism so completely.

A more modern version of fatalism appeared in the form of character John Locke on the blockbuster television series, *Lost*. Locke moved about the island making his decisions based upon his destiny, and his fatalist attitude resulted in a chain of cause and effect events that made television history. Fans of the movie series *The Matrix* will also recognize Morpheus as the fatalist thinker, and of course the great novelist Kurt Vonnegut Jr. wrote about fatalism in *Slaughterhouse-Five*. Fatalism fascinates us—the idea that we are on a fixed path that we cannot deviate from may sound powerless, yet for those who sense the greatness of this predetermined destiny, it can be incredibly empowering and even dangerous.

Without identifying First Cause, though, we can never quite accept any theory that allows for a chain of causal events to occur over which we have no power. We have to first understand that which began it all, and whether or not we were given, by that same First Cause, any say in the ongoing matters of existence.

One theory proposes that the first event and last event are linked in an infinite loop that keeps curling back on itself, a sort of Big Bang leading to End Bang leading to New Big Bang, and on and on. This eliminates the need for a First Cause and allows for an infinite cause and effect chain that just keeps going, like the Energizer Bunny. But of course it doesn't explain why there would be a loop in time and what put it there in the beginning. Yes, everything has to have a beginning, doesn't it?

Necessity

Materialist philosopher Leucippus once said that nothing occurs at random—that everything occurs for a reason and by necessity. Leucippus was one of the first Greek philosophers to develop the "atomism" theory in the end of the 5th century BC. Atomism proposes that everything is made up of indestructible and indivisible atoms, a concept furthered by the works of his pupil, Democritus, which then lead to the idea of determinism and that there is no room in the cosmos for any chance. If every human decision or action is a necessary and inevitable consequence of previous affairs, then there is no chance. Predeterminism is simply the existence of necessity and the absence of chance because the universe conserves information within it and has from the beginning of time, and that there are causal laws that control atoms, and all energy for that matter. Thus, atomic behavior, if fixed, leads to fixed behavior on a grander scale. But are atoms really fixed and do laws of physics control their every aspect? We will look at this in a future chapter.

During the end of the Age of Reason of the late 1700s and into the Age of Enlightenment of the 1800s, there was an explosion of thought, philosophy, science, and intellect throughout much of Europe and the American colonies. One of the schools of thought emerging from this enlightened period was Libertarianism, a metaphysical philosophy that revolved around the issues of free will and determinism. Libertarianism argued that if the universe is deterministic, then free will is illogical, but if agents have free will, then determinism is illogical. This mode of thought was popular with such great thinkers as Robert Kane, Harry Frankfurt, Alfred Mele, and Robert Nozick.

The term was coined in 1789 by William Belsham and evolved into a range of incompatibilist theories that continued into the 19th century. The most noted theories involved the works of Robert Kane, a leading contemporary of free will philosophy. Kane supported the idea that in order for one to act freely, there had to be existing alternative possibilities as a necessary condition. Determinism does not allow for these alternative possible outcomes of choice. In addition, one's actions must be random to be considered a choice. The control of the choice is to be found in the ultimate responsibility of the person making the choice. Kane states in *The Oxford Handbook of Free Will* that the agent behind the free will must be responsible for "anything that is a sufficient reason/condition/cause or motive for the action's occurring." Ultimate control, Kane believed, originated with the agent and the agent alone, and that it is entirely up to the agent to choose from a group of possible choices.

Another more current philosopher, Harry Frankfort, created the P.A.P. theory. The Principle of Alternate Possibilities has three positions:

1. An agent is responsible for an action only if the agent is free.

2. The agent is free if and only if causal determinism is false.

3. Therefore, an agent is responsible for an action only if causal determinism is false.

To Frankfort, a person could only take moral responsibility for an action or choice if and when he could have taken a different course of action, or make a different choice. This makes sense, as if all our choices and actions were predetermined, we would not be morally responsible for them.

The issue of morality plays a powerful role in the arguments for and against free will. For if we do indeed have total control over our choices, then we and we alone must be held responsible for our moral or immoral actions. We cannot blame destiny or fate or God or a blueprint laid down before our birth that dictated each and every move we would make once we were born. Without determinism, and only free will, we would be acting off of our own volition, and not that of a preset series of events that forced us into one choice or another.

What Is Freedom?

What, really, does it mean to be free? We might describe freedom as the ability to move about our existence in total control of the causes we initiate and the effects resulting from them. Or, as Thomas Hobbes, the founding father of political philosophy suggested, freedom is the ability to do what we wish without hindrance or constraint. We can do what we choose, even within the confines of our social, cultural, sexual, and behavioral conditioning, complexes, and needs. This idea was favored by contemporary empiricists, and was expanded to suggest that perhaps freedom was not so much just being able to act without restriction, but to have the power to do, or not do, what one wills. Freedom, then, was an ability restricted to the individual, and not to the will itself, for the will could be tainted with biological, psychological, and social conditions and beliefs, yet a person could still choose to rise above those influences and act out of pure choice.

Freedom, then, can be described as the ability to choose one's own destiny and is incompatible with the idea that destiny is already a given for us without our input. True freedom would have to remove the cause/effect aspect of predeterminism and the God aspect of predestination and leave us and us alone with the power to be First Cause and responsible alone for the effect of that cause. General indeterminism, again, posits that not every event has a cause, so free will and deliberate choice are not predictable from antecedent causes.

Baruch Spinoza, one of the most heralded philosophers of the early modern period, referred to freedom as a kind of "self-determination, where we, the agent, are alone determining our behavior or decisions, and we are not free when others hamper or influence our behavior or decisions." Some argue, though, that our self-determined actions might indeed be influenced by the subconscious and all of its conditionings, beliefs, and concepts that drive our psychological and physiological behavior in ways we may not recognize.

Hume Kant Touch This

David Hume (1711–1776) was a Scottish philosopher and historian, considered one of the founding fathers of Western philosophy. Hume posited that freedom and determinism could find compatibility in the concepts of "liberty and necessity." Necessity he defined as the uniformity and observable in the operations of nature, where similar objects are constantly conjoined together. Liberty is the power of acting, or not acting, according to the determinations of the will. In his book *An Enquiry Concerning Human Understanding*, Hume states that Liberty requires necessity. If one's actions were not necessitate, they would "...have so little in connexion [sic] with motives, inclinations and circumstances, that one does not follow with a certain degree of uniformity from the other." If one's actions are not directly linked to the will, then one's actions can never be free, and instead would be matters of "chance; which is universally allowed not to exist."

Hume argues that in order to be held morally responsible, it is required that our behavior be caused—in other words, necessitated. Actions by nature are "temporary and perishing; and where they proceed not from some cause in the character and disposition of the person who performed them, they can neither redound to his honour, if good; nor infamy, if evil."

The greatest philosopher of the 17th and 18th centuries was no doubt Immanuel Kant (1724–1804), a German who influenced philosophy with his new ideas and perspectives, including his works *Critique of Pure Reason*, *Critique of Practical Reason*, and *Critique of Judgment*. Kant connected freedom with morality and believed that to be free was to simply follow one's own rational principles, and not just desires, and to act in alignment with a higher universal will. To Kant, the idea was to know what our moral duty was, and to act accordingly from that knowledge. His supreme moral principle was "Act only according to that maxim whereby you can at the same time will to be a universal law." He also believed that one should treat humanity, self and others, as an end in itself and not only as a means.

The central tenet of Kant's philosophy was the Categorical Imperative, which stated that because human beings held a special role in the entirety of creation and nature, morality was the one ultimate commandment of reason, so to speak—an imperative from which one's duties, obligations, and actions should originate. An imperative, in turn, proposed a certain action, or inaction, that was necessary. The Categorical Imperative insists that one act on principle, but only on principles that one could will for everyone else in the Universe.

The nitpicking aspect of tearing apart the concepts of determinism and indeterminism, destiny and free will, Fate, and choice all suggest that we are nowhere nearer to understanding which is final truth. Once again, we are left with the pure reality of not knowing our own reality enough to determine whether there was a First Cause, let alone our role in the chain. Without ever doing so, we are left with nothing but ideas, concepts, and theories that hurt the head when looked at in fine detail, and still lead to no particular workable end point that we can say with all certainty is the "real thing."

Philosophers with brains far more potent than this author's brain have still not reached the final conclusion of whether there is pure freedom of will to control one's actions, and thus one's destiny, or a predetermined cause and effect chain of events that is out of one's control. Or both.

This brings to mind another great thinker, William of Occam, a theologian and Franciscan friar who came up with his Occam's Razor, or law of parsimony. This law suggests that one selects the competing hypothesis that makes the fewest new assumptions in terms of postulates or entities. It has erroneously been thought to mean "the correct solution is usually the simplest solution" or, in modern lingo, "keep it simple, stupid." But in the argument of destiny versus free will, those explanations work just as well!

We want to think we are free, but when we make bad choices and the morality issue rears its head, we are quick to blame Fate, destiny, God, and the Devil. When we want to believe there is a blueprint for our lives, we are quick to pitch a fit when we feel we have no choice in the course and direction of our existence. The struggle, then, is to fit the human experience into the confines of pure choice, or pure fate, because we all know the human experience is in itself a mystery wrapped in a riddle. What may feel like a choice freely taken one moment might, three years later, appear to be a piece of a bigger puzzle that is leading to a particular end point. We don't see the pattern until later. Are we the cause of the pattern itself as we make choices, or is the pattern there and we choose how to seek it out?

Maybe religion has the answers that philosophy cannot seem to find.

Two

The Will of God or the Will of Man

"Destiny is no matter of chance. It is a matter of choice. It is not a thing to be waited for, it is a thing to be achieved."
—William Jennings Bryan

"Life is like a game of cards. The hand you are dealt is determinism; the way you play it is free will."
—Jawaharial Nehru

"Man was predestined to have free will."
—Anonymous

God willing, this book will be finished on time. And yet, it is my own will that pushes me, the author, to beat the deadline. Some may argue that the two are the same, but others find distinctions between the will of the divine and the choices men make—and women.

In an August 2010 article for *USA Today* by Tom Krattenmaker titled "What if the End Isn't Near?" opinion polls claim that more than half the American public expects the end times to come; some of course believe it will come sooner than others. Many of these are Christians who await the literal translation of the Book of Revelation, the visions of St. John the Divine, which tells of the unspeakable horrors we can expect before the return of the Christ. The destiny of the world, it seems, is set in stone for the millions, perhaps billions, of believers. They simply do not have a choice in the matter.

Religion has always been about doctrine, laws, rules, and prophecies. God, or the deity in question, has a will for humankind, and a final destiny for them. But those who choose not to follow the will of God will pay a price. World religions struggle with the concepts of destiny and choice just as the leadership of these religions struggle to keep some kind of authoritarian power over their flock, yet let the flock have a little bit of freedom to keep them happy and distracted.

Christianity and Will

Christianity is no different, as the *USA Today* article continues, describing a new breed of Christians who are not willing to accept the end game without putting up a good fight against worldwide destruction. This is in direct opposition to the end timers who seem to salivate over visions of death and doom and gloom, visions that correspond with the promised salvation and destiny of those without sin (if you can find any!). But the newest generation of evangelicals and other Christians may take their destiny into their own hands. Krattenmaker says, "If end-times acceptance is losing cred- ibility among the new generation of Jesus followers—and many signs say it is—this is good news to us all." He goes on to say that this new generation can "bet on a supernatural rescue for them- selves and their kind and wait for cataclysm. Or they can dedicate themselves to compassionate action to alleviate suffering and in- justice." Finally he asks, "Which would their savior have them do?"

Western religious traditions find a way to walk between the worlds of destiny and free will by assigning the ultimate power to God, yet offering choice to the humans who will suffer the con- sequences should they not follow God's will. In other words, it's God's way or the highway—to hell. Free will carried with it harsh penalties, often stoning or crucifixion, or worse.

For Christians, the idea of predestination or predetermination comes from the belief that much of human life has been figured out before hand by a fatherly God who controls much of their behavior and circumstances. What God has ordained, will come to pass, no matter the course of human actions and behaviors in between. The end destination would be the same, either eternity in heaven with the Lord, the fiery pits of hell, or walking in the dead zone of purgatory. Of course, one did have a choice as to where he or she would end up. Follow church doctrine and a destiny in heaven is a sure thing. Make mistakes or commit a sin and that course might change, allowing for some flexibility after all (although not the kind one might want, considering the consequence!).

St. Augustine of Hippo is probably the best-known figure as- sociated with divine providence and the adoption of this doctrine throughout the Catholic world. Divine providence is the action and activity of God in the world, with God being omniscient and hav- ing knowledge of the future. God is also, in a sense, a provider who watches out for the world, watches over it. The word *providence* actually is translated from the Latin *providential*, which means "foresight, knowledge of the future, prudence...."

Divine providence allows God to be all-knowing and all-powerful, always acting for the best of the world and its inhabitants. Yet this is not consistent with reality, where evil is allowed to exist. Thus the element of free will was added on to allow for evil to exist as a choice made by mankind. As St. Augustine believed, God moves our wills to do good, but God does not diminish our freedom. If He did, we would not be motivated to work toward the promised salvation. There is no conflict between God's will and our freedom.

St. Thomas Aquinas believed that God as a creator was First Cause, and that God's activity as First Cause was the cause of our freedom. In *Summa Contra Gentiles*, he expounds that God alone moves the "creaturely will" and does so without force or violence. God can move it from within, thus giving us some autonomy to be a free agent. We are not puppets violently manipulated by a controlling God force. Both Aquinas and Augustine believed that God was without sin, and was perfectly holy and all good. Sin, then, had to be a pure act of free human will. But to these great thinkers, it was not. It was still a part of the omniscience of God and His will. How could this be reconciled?

God and Suffering

God, ultimately, to the Judeo-Christian world, allows for both sin and suffering as a part of His plan, fully engaged with humanity as it struggles to overcome both sin and suffering, yet allowing us to take an active role in the defeat of sin and suffering. In a sense, God is like King Arthur encouraging his Knights of the Round Table to live according to the laws of chivalrous action, to do good and spread good, to defeat evil. God, like King Arthur, invites us to cooperate with His will and help guide creation to an ultimate destiny and perfection. And in order to reach that state of perfection, there must be evil to overcome, and suffering as well. "We know that in everything, God works for good for those who love Him," says Romans 8:28. But if you choose to not love God and go against His will, sin and suffering become a part of your reality. St. Catherine of Siena reminds us in John Wesley's *On Divine Providence* that "Some rebel against what happens to them, but God does nothing without the salvation of man in mind." And Julian of Norwich believed and wrote in *Revelations of Divine Love* that "All shall be well, all shall be well, and all manner of things shall be well."

If these confusing statements, which try to find a precarious balance between destiny and free will, divine control and human freedom, seem to be a cop-out, it is only because this battle between the two philosophies has never been finally put to rest—and perhaps it never will be. Religion continues to be at the forefront of trying to rectify the two, and explain via their respective doctrines how they can both co-exist, while still making sure that believers respect authority and the doctrine itself.

Many denominations, such as Calvinism, believe that before the act of creation, God had already determined the fate of the entire universe. This kind of predestination suggests that some will be saved and others not, depending on the fate the Creator set for them as individuals. Monotheistic systems such as Christianity, Judaism, and Islam believed in this type of determinism because of the attributes of omniscience to God. An eternal, omniscient God would be one who knows all—past, present, and future—and thus knows ahead of time what will happen. But the question remains: If God knows the future, does God also control every single aspect of it?

In an article titled "Researchers Probe Whether, Why, 'Free Will' Exists," by Amy Green for the online news service Religion News Service, we learn that scientists, philosophers, and theologians from all over the world will have a gathering of ideas to discuss what factors lead us to do what we do. To the tune of a $4.4 million grant, these great minds will look at free will and destiny as well as genetics and environmental issues.

Much of the debate involves asking questions such as these: Does God give humans free choice to turn away from decisions and actions that will harm them? Does God know how everything turns out in the end? Or is it all up to us humans? One of those involved in the study is Kevin Timpe, an associate professor of philosophy at Northwest Nazarene University in Nampa, Idaho. Timpe is also the author of *Free Will: Sourcehood and its Alternatives* and hopes to discuss the difference between knowing what someone will do, and causing them to do it: "I know what my wife is going to order when I take her to certain restaurants just because I know her very well. But I also think my wife is freely choosing to order."

Thus, can an omniscient God also co-exist with human free will? Another participant, author Norman Geisler, who also writes about free will, believes that the idea of free will is compatible with biblical teachings and the doctrine of original sin. He points to Adam's decision to eat from the tree of knowledge as one that had to have been made freely, or else God would be responsible for all evil in the world: "The Bible constantly affirms that man is free… that he can choose his destiny…." We cannot blame God (or the devil it seems) for the choices we make, something a lot of politicians, athletes, and preachers like to do as of late.

All religions allow for suffering and evil. The Western traditions seem to affirm that God allows suffering and evil to test the faith of humans, or as a form of discipline. But these religions also often blame the devil for said evils, thus removing some of the responsibility from the humans who commit the negative acts. Contrast this with the Eastern concept, seen in Hinduism and Buddhism, of man's suffering originating from his own ignorance, the result of past karma to be worked out in each successive lifetime. To the Hindus, Buddhists, Jains, and Sikhs, liberation or "Moksha" is the final destiny of humanity. This is the release from the karmic cycle of birth and death and rebirth, and comes with the achievement of a state of perfection and immortality. Thus, the less suffering you inflict on others, the quicker you get to the final state of liberation or freedom.

For the Western traditions, heaven and hell may therefore be the liberation, although these are final states upon death—final destinies with no room for improvement. Yet Christianity and Hinduism share a common belief that life on this earthly level is a form of hell, a place of suffering and lessons to be learned, usually the hard way, with hopes of some final far-off salvation that will end the cycle.

But always, destiny is a place of either eternal freedom, or eternal imprisonment. It all depends on the choices made along the way.

Moral Evil

There is, in fact, an argument from moral evil known as the "free-will defense," which takes the position that the very existence of evil disproves the existence of God. Evil is the result of the free will of moral agents. The argument progresses as such:

··· *God, if He exists, is omnipotent, omniscient, and benevolent.*

··· *If God is these things, than there would be no moral evil in the world.*

··· *There is moral evil in the world.*

··· *Therefore, God does not exist.*

Although this may sound a bit black and white, the focus is on the nature of God as all-powerful, all-knowing, and all-good, which then leaves little room for the existence of evil. Thus, we must now find a reason why God allows evil to exist.

Is God neutral? If so, then the onus of responsibility falls entirely upon us as to whether evil exists or not. And thus, our destiny is entirely in our hands. A neutral God would not care whether we went to Heaven or Hell, found liberation or imprisonment. A neutral God almost nullifies the belief in destiny outright. Free will is all that exists.

But what if God instead is all-knowing and all-powerful, and yet allows for evil for a specific reason—one that we don't recognize or understand? If evil is something we are allowed to take part in as a test of our own personal evolution and morality, then God can be all-good, knowing that His will for us is to move freely toward the highest and best destiny possible. This bridges the gaps between the black-and-white thinking of either total predestination, or total free choice. God cares, and allows us to make the bigger decisions, because if He did not, he would not care!

The whole point of life, mystics tell us, is to grow and become and aspire toward a higher way of being and thinking, a progression toward a divine perfection that may be our final destiny, with a billion or so different choices we can make along the way to get there. If God created all good and moral people who never slipped up, what would be the point of life?

Jocelyn Bell Burnell, a physicist who discovered pulsars, is quoted as saying that there is a possible resolution to the ageless questions of why God allows suffering, and does God care? In the book *Nobel Prize Women in Science*, by Sharon Bertch McGrayne, Burnell states, "If the world is not run by God, then the calamities that occur cannot be blamed on God. Perhaps God decided that we are responsible adults that should be given a free hand and allowed to get on with life without interference...." She continues by saying that God exerts influence in the world, but He does so through us, through people, their attitudes and behaviors, and their healing and reconciliation. She even ties this in with the "randomness of uncertainty" that is found in everything in modern physics, a liberating notion that can free us from the black and white thinking of just and unjust, cause and effect: "Pain is not a part of a Grand Design and will not come to a purposeful ending unless we work at it to ensure that it does."

In other words, God's will are the parameters we are given, and free will is the direction within those parameters we choose to take. A useful analogy might be imagining we live in a big box, and the boundaries of that box are the limitations God has given us to work with. We can go anywhere in the box we want, to this wall or that, that corner or the other one, or stay in the center.

Much of this argument has to do with the idea of just how mutable the future is. If the entire future, down to every detail, is set in stone, all the way to the point of death, then life itself seems pointless, unless the purpose is something we are not wise enough to discern. Yet this robot-like existence does not sit well with any religion. The presence of a deity, or a God, automatically suggests that someone or something put us here for a reason. And that reason is our ultimate destiny.

There is another way to look at predestination. Chinese Buddhism translates predestination as *yuanfen*, which simply implies that we take the word literally. *Pre* means before. Thus, predestination means "before destiny," and suggests that there is a linear fashion to our lives in which some things are bound to happen. *Bound to happen*, though, does not mean that they *will* happen. And this explanation leaves out the need for a God. The destiny of events is part of a mutable universe, one in which things can change, and changes can create a different series of events that are *bound to happen*, thus leading to a different destiny!

Once again, it all comes down to the definition of God. If God is able to see into the past, present, and future, then that means that God knows the future. Therefore, the future is already a given in the mind of God. The caveat here is that just because God has the ability to see into the future does not necessarily mean God has actually determined the future and the destinies of all that are moving toward it. One is determinism, the other predestination.

Even within Christianity, there are arguments about the types of destinies God offers humanity, and also whether or not God gives us any room for maneuvering within those destinies. Depending on denomination, some Christians believe that the word of God and the will of God are all there is and that there is nothing you or I can do about it. This rigidity of thinking is most in line with fundamentalist thought, and the more extreme systems of belief that hold up to a controlling and punishing God the Father, one who must be feared and obeyed at all times.

The other side of the coin offers a less-harsh view of destiny, with many Christians instead believing that God is sovereign, but in His infinite wisdom offered us the gift of free will as a way to allow us to determine our own future. This means that upon birth, destiny is mutable, depending upon the decided actions of the person along the road of life. God watches over, but does not crack the whip. Sins are paid for in one way or the other, in a type of karma, for people must eventually answer to the final judge and jury for what they've accomplished and what they've done (or, on the other hand, what they didn't do).

There are actually two types of predestination at work here, both with entirely different outcomes.

One type states that our lot in life—our destiny—is determined by God before we are born and we have no say in it. God has all the cards and plays them as He wants to. It's all a done deal by the time we come tumbling out of the womb and into existence.

The other states that destiny is a result of free will choices made along the way. It's like having a choice between vacation spots to spend your summer in, and a zillion different ways to get to either locale.

There are two extremes operation within these two types. One is a "univocal" conception of free will, which allows for a Creator who gives humans absolute free will. The system of creation itself allows for it, whether divine in nature or the result of evolution. The other end of these extremes suggests that the Creator exercises absolute will over creation and is the ultimate cause of all decisions. This leaves no room for human will or evolution outside of the actual will of the Creator. Any will on the part of humans is imagined.

The "equivocal" concept allows for a Creator who also allows for individual choice. Human will is free but determined by the Creator. So human will allows for personal responsibility, but not in an absolute sense. Human decisions might then be actual expressions of divine will, and that human will is dependent upon the will of the Creator, but not entirely beholden to it. It could be said that humans are responsible in their actions, but their actions are not original, which is the foundation of Original Sin, where we are all born into a state of being entirely helpless to sin no matter what we do or who our parents are. Sin comes with us just as our belly buttons do.

Other Traditions

Islam simplifies this a bit by allowing human will to be powerless without the help of Allah, but free from that Original Sin. Everything that happens then is the will of Allah, but "Allah changeth not the condition of a people until they change what is in their hearts." For a religion many hold to be so extremist, this seems like a very agreeable concept in contrast with Original Sin, where you can't win for losing!

Other religious traditions uphold different views. Eastern Orthodoxy supports the view that without grace, no effort on behalf of man is worth a damn. Human effort has no power but for the grace imparted upon those efforts, which will determine their success or failure. With grace and effort, a man can progress toward his goal, but lacking grace, the efforts fall flat.

Lutherans believe that they are on the road to promised and predestined salvation. Martin Luther taught in his *On the Bondage of the Will* that by grace and faith salvation is promised. It is a gift from God, and not the effects of good works, removing the ego and responsibility from man. God, in Lutheran thought, lays down beforehand the works we should do and the path we should walk to achieve that salvation.

Another Protestant denomination, Arminianism, believes that God predicts ahead of time who will be saved, but still allows the individual the choice of being saved or not.

There seems to be ample evidence for conflicting beliefs in the Old Testament and New Testament regarding God's will and that of man.

Destiny and the Bible

- "Many are called, but few are chosen." (Matthew 22:14)
- "Before I formed you in the womb I knew you, before you were born I set you apart...." (Jeremiah 1:5)
- "In love, he predestined us to adoption as sons through Jesus Christ to Himself, according to the kind intention of his will." (Ephesians 1:5)
- "I will have mercy on whom I have mercy, and I will have compassion on whom I have compassion." (Romans 9:15)
- "For by grace you have been saved through faith and that not of yourselves: it is the gift of God, not of works, lest anyone should boast." (Ephesians 2:8)
- "For truly in this city there were gathered together against Your holy servant Jesus, whom You anointed, both Herod and Pontius Pilate, along with the Gentiles and the peoples of Israel, to do whatever Your hand and Your purpose predestined to occur." (Acts: 4:27–28)
- "The Lord killeth, and maketh alive: he bringeth down to the grave, and bringeth up. The Lord maketh poor, and maketh rich: he bringeth low, and lifteth up." (1 Samuel: 6–7)

Free Will and the Bible

··· "According to your faith, let it be to you." (Matthew 9:29)

··· "If you abide in Me, and My words abide in you, you will ask what you desire, and it shall be done for you." (John 15:7)

··· "No one takes my life away from me. I give it up of my own free will." (John 10:18)

··· "And if it seem evil unto you to serve the LORD, choose you this day whom ye will serve; whether the gods which your fathers served that were on the other side of the flood, or the gods of the Amorites, in whose land ye dwell: but as for me and my house, we will serve the LORD." (Joshua 24:15)

··· "Envy thou not the oppressor, and choose none of his ways." (Proverbs 3:31)

··· "Therefore to him that knoweth to do good, and doeth it not, to him it is sin." (James 4:17)

··· "I tell you the truth, if you have faith as small as a mustard seed, you can say to this mountain, 'Move from here to there'" and it will move.'" (Matthew 17:20)

··· "The truth shall make you free." (John 8:32)

··· "He who believes and is baptized will be saved; but he who does not believe will be condemned." (Mark 16:16)

Reform Judaism appears to have introduced the concept of God being both omnipotent and omniscient long after the Old Testament texts were composed. Perhaps influenced by Neo-Platonic thought, many Orthodox, Conservative, and Reform Jews use the existence of free will to deny that one's destiny is predetermined.

God may have knowledge of the future and what people may or may not choose to do, but will not control those decisions. Thus, a saying by Rabbi Akiva in the *Pirkei Avoth* sums this belief up by stating, "Everything is foreseen; yet free will is given...." Whether or not God can be said to be omniscient matters not. Man has free will.

Jewish philosophy ascribes free will to the human soul, calling it *neshama*, or breath. But, it is the *yechida*, the part of our soul that is connected to God, that allows us to make the choices we freely make, and because God is not bounded by cause and effect, the *neshama* is still under some divine direction. Having a soul allows for free will, but again, only the soul connection with the deity makes it happen.

Judaism in general understands that humans are created in God's image. As God's chosen people, those of the Jewish faith believe in divine providence, or *Hashgachah Protis*, which translates to the divine supervision of the individual (Orthodox Jews believe that God directs all of creation) but also a collective destiny, or *Olam-Ha-Ba*, meaning "world to come," but they place less emphasis on how their behaviors and actions effect them after death. Instead, moral choices, promises, and agreements or covenants with God are more about this life, with obvious reward and punishment meted accordingly. Good actions should be taken for the good of all, and not just for the reward of the afterlife. A moral life in Judaism is not for the sole purpose of gaining good favor in heaven. Thus, a life is not necessarily preordained so much as it is given a strict set of boundaries that, if lived within, will lead to this world to come beyond death.

Islamic belief also includes a divine preordainment, or decree of Allah, and that nothing that occurs in the world, good or evil, does so without the permission of Allah. But Muslim theologians also state that free will plays a role in human behavior, for each human has the choice to act responsibly in accordance with what has been decreed by Allah, written in the "Preserved Tablet," or "al-Lawh al-Mahfuz." Events may be set in stone, but actions and behaviors are not, thus placing a great deal of importance on making responsible choices and being prepared to face the consequences. There are always consequences to those who deny Allah, His messengers, angels, and teachings. Like Christians and Jews, it all comes down to the day of divine judgment, when each man and woman will be held accountable for the choices they made and, at that time, be given their final destiny.

Some Islamic scholars believe that Allah controls every aspect of human behavior, leaving no room at all for free will and choice. People might believe they are acting of their own accord, but in reality Allah has it all planned out in advance and it must be the will of Allah that anything should happen at all. *Mashallah* means that Allah has ordained what will happen to a believer. Sunni Islam's foundation exists upon the principles of predestination. Allah is perfect, all-knowing. Allah has foretold all that will happen before the universe was created and well into the future, and Allah not only created all people, but their behaviors and actions as well. As for evil, it happens only because Allah wills it, and we are not to try to understand the deeper reasons why.

Shiites offer more room for free will, with personal responsibility determining one's fate on Judgment Day. How near one is to Allah and the will of Allah, determines what a person can do, and if one turn's his back on Allah, he will pay dearly for it in the end. The concept of *bada* affirms that Allah has not predetermined humanity's fate, but can *change that fate* if needed.

The notion of a Day of Resurrection in the Islamic belief system encourages that one measures his individual deeds and actions against the final judgment, or *yawm al-qiyamah*, when every deceased soul's deeds will be weighed on a scale called *mizan*, before Allah. One's actions during the physical life, then, determine the destiny of the soul after death, similar to the notion of the final Judgment Day of Judeo-Christian belief.

Eastern Religious Concepts

To the Buddhism of the East, *karma* is the word of choice to describe a type of free will that allows one to make the right choices and be rewarded for doing so. Karma comes from the Sanskrit root word *Kri*, or "action." Karma is a type of moral law following linear cause and effect. An individual thus determines the path of karma through the actions, deeds, and words of his or her choosing. Each action has a particular influence, and thus a particular consequence. This is not fate, not a preplanning of a life by an external deity. The Buddhist scripture "Dhammapada" (often ascribed to Buddha himself) states: "All that we are is a result of what we have thought. It is founded on our thoughts and made up of our thoughts." Thoughts lead to actions, which lead to karmic cause and effect.

The Buddhist belief in reincarnation and the 10 realms of being that a human can aspire to leave plenty of room for free will. With the state of Bodhisattva, an enlightened one as the Buddha, there is a destiny of sorts that a human can ascend to—a level of "achievement" that can be looked at as an end goal. But from the lower human level, and those levels even lower, to the top of the enlightenment chain, there are a whole lot of different paths and choices an individual can make. Those choices will of course dictate what level the individual comes back in the next time around. Karma is the driving force that decides how close to Buddhahood one gets in the next state of being.

Buddhism accepts that both destiny as determinism and free will can exist side by side. What is absent from this philosophy is the outer, exterior agent that governs the destiny and choices of human beings. Buddha stated that there is free action, and there is even retribution, but according to the "Dhammapada" there is no agent "that passes out from one set of momentary elements into another one, except the connection of those elements." There is, always in Buddhism, a middle path or road, and with destiny and free will that is no different. Buddhists call it *pratitya-samutpada*, which is a Sanskrit term translated as "arising from inter-dependence." This has touches of the concept of karma, which in Buddhism focuses on the cause and effect of one's actions, thoughts and behaviors in this present life.

Mind you, there is no absolute free will, mainly because we humans cannot do anything and everything we want to. We may not be physically capable of flying without aid of a machine, no matter how much we will it! But to Buddhists, moral progress and compassionate action serve as the catalysts for choices that will, hopefully, lead to more moral and more compassionate choices and actions.

Hinduism is the oldest of the major religious traditions. Hindus also believe in karma, but with a different spin. To the Hindu, karma determines the destiny of a person in future lives. Again, Buddhism focuses on this present life, but Hinduism takes the thoughts, choices, and actions of a person and ascribes them to future lives as well. The six schools of Hindu thought, known as *astika*, vary in degrees as to the question of free will and choice, but the most notable is the Vedantic belief that free will is influenced by cause and effect. Swami Vivekananda notably stated in *Freedom: The Complete Works of Swami Vivekananda* that there cannot be absolute free will because will describes what we know within our own universe, "moulded by conditions of time, space and causality." Thus, to truly acquire absolute free will, one would have to transcend this universe and all of its physical limitations and laws. He also believed that men who blamed fate for their actions and choices were "cowards and fools," because of the power of conscious choice humans were given.

In other words, we seem to have a kind of free will, but one that is entirely governed by the laws of the universe we live in. The parameters come pre-set. To have total freedom is to go beyond the limitations of our universe. Karma allows us the opportunity to be responsible and own up to past actions, and do better in the present so that we may one day get a future reward of more freedom of will.

Hinduism believes that the *atman* or soul will leave the body upon death, and be reincarnated in a new body in a continuous cycle of birth, death, and rebirth, or *samsara*. The goal is to be reincarnated in the highest form possible, which is determined by the actions and deeds of the current life. Thus, free will leads to a specific destiny, whether it is being reborn as a plant, an animal, or a human being. Ultimately, Hindus want off the continuous wheel of samsara, to reach a point of merging with the absolute, or *Brahman*. This release, *Moksha,* is only achievable through *dharma*, or right action. One who takes the path of right action can eventually achieve this freedom from the cycle of samsara, and therefore achieve the ultimate destiny based upon lifetimes of good and positive free choices.

The common thread between most major religious traditions seems to be this: There is a destiny that one can aspire to, if one makes the best use of the free will given. Think of planning to run a marathon, all 26.2 miles of it. The marathon is the destiny, the end goal, the result of all the choices that we make to get to that destiny. Those choices can include training; not training; doing a 5K, then a 10K, then a half marathon; or deciding in the end not to do the marathon at all, because who wants to run 26.2 miles only to possibly lose one's bodily functions at the finish line?

Whether that free will is given from God, or just something we are "born into" as humans with brains, minds, and consciences, the path we choose to take determines the final outcome of heaven or hell, samsara or release, Buddhahood or another go-around of the same old, same old. The constant grappling that religious traditions deal with when trying to reconcile free will and fate is almost funny, when one takes a good look at the overwhelming nitpicking of philosophies and theories (much of which this author felt the need to spare you from).

Atheists ascribe to the belief that it is all about choice, and only free will exists, because to believe in a fate or destiny is to accept the possibility of divine intervention. But it would be hard pressed to find anyone who can honestly say that his or her life has been free from some sort of divine providence, guidance, serendipity, or synchronicity, or the pull toward some particular, if not entirely knowable, end result.

Did God desire for me to be a writer? Certainly I have been writing since early childhood, and it has been a driving force in my life. Yet I have also made choices that continued to move me toward a career as a writer. I can say that, yes, at times, I felt that "God" was bringing people and opportunities to me at the right times, and certainly the way some aspects of my career have "fallen into place" as if by magic speak of divine providence. But I also work my ass off. Perhaps Joseph Campbell, the great mythologist and comparative religion expert, was correct when he said we should follow our bliss, and doors would be open to us. From my personal experience, I can truly say that there have been times when I knew divine providence was moving in my world, and other times when I made choices that went against my "gut" that caused me great pain and misery.

Those with a strong proclivity toward a particular religion may find that the doctrine of destiny and free will allows them the comfort of not having to think for themselves about the two. If you are Christian, you believe this. If Hindu, you believe this. Yet the actions and behaviors of so many people seem to bear little resemblance to these teachings about taking responsibility for our choices, choices that will lead to reward or punishment, both in this life and the next (and the next and the next and the next). Looking at all the violence, abuse, and misery in the world causes one to pause and wonder if we have given up any hope of a collective destiny that serves the higher good, and just settled into the "my-free-will or the highway" mode of thinking.

If there is a God watching over us, determining our fate depending on our behavior down here in the trenches, then perhaps we better watch what we choose. And even if there isn't, we still have the immediate law of cause and effect to deal with. Our choices

lead to consequences, which lead to more choices and more consequences, and in the end, that becomes our destiny.

Either way, it behooves us to act a little bit better, doesn't it?

Fig. 2A/Fig. 2B

The Japanese and Chinese (simplified) symbols for destiny.

Three

Written in the Stars:
The Destiny of Divination

"A wise man shall overrule his stars, and have a
greater influence upon his own content than all the
constellations and planets of the firmament."
—Jeremy Taylor

"The signs of the zodiac are karmic patterns; the planets are the
looms; the will is the weaver."
—Unknown

"It is not in the stars to hold our destiny, but in ourselves."
—William Shakespeare

Many believe that fortune-telling is truly the world's oldest profession. In Bangkok, Thailand, a CNN reporter named Greg Jorgensen decided to visit three different fortune-tellers and report on their accuracy. In "Tempting Fate: Bangkok Fortune Tellers Reviewed," a June 3, 2010, CNN-GO! special report, Jorgensen, who considers himself "highly skeptical," visited a palm reader, a numerologist, and a Tarot reader to see if his destiny was written on his hand, in the numbers, or in the cards. The end results were varied. Jorgensen stated about palm reading that the art is more about "a way to read a person's character, not so much to forecast what is ahead for them." He found his reader's comments generic at best. His numerology reading was vague, too, except for being told the exact year and age he would die (88 years of age in the year 2063). As for the Tarot, Jorgensen wasn't blown away, but did give Tarot reading a modicum of credibility due to the fact that you pick your own cards, thus making it easier to get something out of the reading.

Three fortune-tellers, three vague readings. Only one went out on a limb to give an exact date that could later be verified. And still, the power of belief might be called into play when someone tells you the exact time you will die. You just might believe it into happening. Choice? Or destiny?

Palmistry

In Thailand, palm readers are called *mor doo*. The art of palmistry, or chromancy, interprets the lines of the palm and is generally considered pure pseudoscience. With roots that can be traced back to India (Hindu astrology), China (iChing) and gypsy cultures, palm reading evaluates both a person's character traits and his or her future by looking specifically at the lines of the palm. Some palmistry traditions also look at the shapes and sizes of the fingers, fingernails, and skin patterns, but basic palm reading focuses on the following:

1. *The left hand dominates the right brain and shows the person's past. The left hand is the realm of the inner person, the anima, and the yin/receptive aspects of the feminine.*

2. The right hand controls the left brain and its world of logic, intellect, and reason. This is the realm of the outer persona, the objective self, and the yang aspect of the masculine. It is the domain of the future.

There are beliefs that various hand shapes are associated with the elements of earth, air, water, and fire, but for most people, like Jorgesen, who go to see a palm reader, the main concern are the lines.

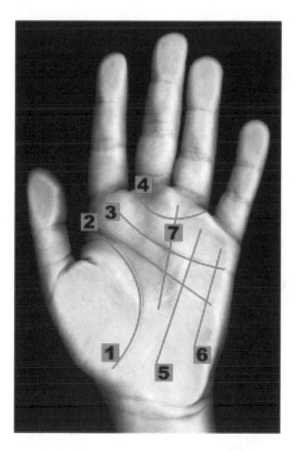

Fig. 3-A

1. The Heart Line: This is the major line during a reading, as it indicates all matters of the heart, emotions, love, romance, and even heart health.
2. The Head Line: This line represents the mind and learning styles, communication skills, intellect, and thought processing.
3. The Life Line: This line is fraught with controversy because it represents physical health, well-being, vitality, and energy, but also shows cataclysmic changes and events in a person's life. It once was believed to indicate length of life, but this is not a widely accepted belief in modern palmistry.

Perhaps, with regard to this book, the one line we should most be interested in is the Fate Line, also known as the Line of Destiny. This line is directly tied to a person's unique life path, including the challenges and obstacles one will meet with along that path. The Fate Line also indicates circumstances beyond a person's control, including major changes in career, relationships, and health.

Markings along the Fate Line are said to show specific events that have, or will, occur that will be life-altering. Because Fate is at the helm, the events are not chosen by the person, but experienced without choice, but some palm readers believe instead that it might indicate choices one will make that have major consequences. Once again, even with a person's palm, we have a battle between a fixed determinism and cause-and-effect free will.

Lines of Life and Destiny

I feel that I am a wonderful example of free will: When I was studying Palmistry in my mid-30s, I saw on my Life Line on my right hand (what I put out to the world) a broken line that picked up again. Generally, a broken life line means dramatic health problems. On my left hand (what I feel emotionally), the life line was not broken, but complete. By that time in my life, I had stopped using alcohol and drugs. I vowed that I would mitigate the break and slowly changed my life: I gave up smoking, changed my thinking to positive ways (I was born depressed and it runs in both sides of my family), changed my health/diet routines, and developed myself more emotionally.

Gradually, over the years I could see a line develop that connected the sides of the broken Life Line. And...in 2002, I had the most wonderful cerebral aneurysm hemorrhage! After it happened, I felt so peaceful and complete (and slept) until I was taken to the hospital and had surgery to block off the bleeding. I remember telling the doctor that nothing bad was going to happen to me. After three days, I was home, on and off, for three weeks. I know it was my body, and the universe, telling me that I needed rest (I had not had that much time off since age 14) and, because I have an understanding husband, I used the time for my spiritual development, learned how to balance myself better, and write again, like I used to. I've had no long-term effects from this, and am grateful for the experience. I feel that I used my free will to prepare myself and, therefore, changed my fate/destiny.

I feel that it helps us to tune into and understand the vibrations of ourselves and the universe. I interpret them for my clients, for other people important in my life (including our cat), and myself because I feel that if you are prepared/forewarned, then people can go with the flow instead of struggling so much with it.

—Alexandra Andrews, PhD, is a spiritual psychic, teacher, and founder of the Alexandra Institute (*www.alexandrainstitute.org*).

Palmistry is to this day considered a non-science because of the lack of any kind of verification or controlled research. But millions of people still seek out the help of a palm reader, hoping to find in the lines of their hands the answers to difficult questions or the promise of a bright future. Of all the divination methods to be discussed in this chapter, palmistry alone may have more potential "clout" as a marker for destiny because of genetics. The human hand could be said to be a physical marker of specific characteristics, gifts, and talents that lead to specific life choices that in turn make up a destined path, just as DNA governs the physical look and shape, as well as line length, of the human palm.

With palmistry or any other form of divination involving human body parts, such as cranium shape, eye color and shape, even face part placement, we can reach for a connection to the very "stuff" that makes us human to begin with. For those systems involving numbers and the positioning of the stars, or cards chosen from a deck, or stones cast upon a silk cloth, the connections are all based upon claims of ancient knowledge, wisdom, and interpretation.

Numerology

Though science does not look upon numerology as a serious field, it is a very old one. Using numbers and the corresponding letters of the alphabet, numerologists can chart the course of a person's life and determine their strong and week character traits and behaviors. Numerology recognizes the occult symbolism of numbers, but most people would be surprised to know just how much influence numbers have on our lives in a more scientific sense. Everything, as Pythagoras once said, comes down to number.

For those who seek to determine the path of a human life, these ancient systems link aspects of astrology, astronomy, alchemy, chemistry, and sacred geometry to create a blueprint based upon the birth name of a person, which was believed to have just as great a significance as the time, date, and location of birth (more to come on astrology later).

Numerology has its roots in the ancient cultural beliefs of the Babylonians, Sumerians, Greeks, and Egyptians, among others, and some of the beliefs have even infiltrated the great Western religious belief systems, as well as those of the far East. It seems no religion or culture has been untouched by the idea that numbers mean more than just what they measure. Mathematicians and philosophers throughout the last 2,000 years have attributed numbers with profound and often sacred power, as the universal language given to humans by God, as St. Augustine of Hippo believed.

Despite today being relegated to pseudoscience, numerology continues to fascinate people who refuse to believe that just because it isn't provable, doesn't mean it does not work. In fact, many people swear by their "numbers."

The problem is, there are different systems of numerology, and different ways to interpret the resulting numbers associated with one's birth name. There are also different alphabets that the different number systems corresponded with, such as the Arabic, Hebrew, or Greek. So, depending upon which system/alphabet a reader utilizes, you might end up with four different readings from four different readers, and even if they all agreed on your master/ destiny number, the most critical number that dictates the course of your life, you must then wade through spins and biases of interpretation. Among the methods of calculation and interpretation are the Japanese, the Arabic, the Phonetic, the Indian, the Chaldean, and the Pythagorean.

This is why it is so hard for true science to accept numerology. There is little consistency in the systems that exist, or have existed over time, to fit the dictates of a true scientific method that begs for repeatability and verification. But still, there is a part of our nature that knows, on a more subjective and intuitive level, the powerful connection between us and the numbers we are immersed in. (Read more about this in my book *11:11—The Time Prompt Phenomenon: The Meaning Behind Mysterious Signs, Sequences, and Synchronicities*, written with Larry Flaxman).

Numbers and Fate

Whether you believe in a set fate, a moldable destiny, or somewhere in between, mathematics and science have proven one thing to be true: All things are energy. Quantum physics has recently discovered that at the base of an atom is not solid matter, as once thought. At the core of the building blocks of life are actually frozen light particles.

Energy is not created but has always been there. We can harness, redirect, or modify energy, but the basis of it remains the same. Energy follows predictable patterns and cycles but it is also malleable. Armed with the truth that our world is constructed from energy proves the theory that some things are indeed set as fate but there is also the opportunity to shape our destiny.

Many of us often feel like a ship being tossed around in the sea with no control over life's direction. Energy cannot be seen, so it is difficult to recognize the patterns within and around us. Numbers are the language of energy and can give us a window into the world of energy. Mathematics and numbers have always represented the unseen world of energy and many scientists have changed the world through their mathematical discoveries.

What if you could understand your own energetic pattern and learn how to harness and mold it as you desire? Your life would shift from being lost at sea to being the captain in full control of your ship.

All numbers in existence are created using the digits 0–9. Using the science of numbers (numerology), these digits represent the base energy patterns that make up our world, and you are one or more of these patterns. Knowing your pattern is like knowing the ingredients of your recipe. Your date of birth is your recipe. The individual digits in your date of birth are your ingredient list, and the sum of those digits is what is created when those ingredients are combined. For example, if your birth date is January 12, 1990, the digits add up to 23 (1 + 1 + 2 + 1 + 9 + 9 + 0 = 23). You then add 2 + 3 to get the final number: 5.

Our energetic pattern is set at birth but how we choose to use it is our destiny. Although you are a specific energetic pattern that remains the same at its basis, you can focus your energy in any way that you wish. A cake is a cake, but you can bake it in whatever shape you wish and decorate it is anyway you'd like.

Knowing your energetic patterns shifts your life from chaos to clarity. There are many different ways to self-awareness and understanding but the numbers in your date of birth are like the code of the soul. Understanding your soul's code means the difference between being pulled along by fate and becoming the creator of your own destiny. Unlock your destiny using the power of numbers.

1 Keywords: verbal self-expression, initiate, action, ambitious, determined, pioneering, aggressive

2 Keywords: contrast, balance, cooperation, sensitive, intuitive, supportive, co-dependent

3 Keywords: analytical, intelligent, humorous, social, sensitive, observant, critical

4 Keywords: endurance, progress, foundation, practical, organization, solid, stable, materialistic

5 Keywords: loving, sensitive, irregular, artistic, freedom-seeking, passionate, uncertain

6 Keywords: creative, responsible, nurturing, home-loving, peace-maker, doting, worry-wart, people-pleaser, hostess, gossipy

7 Keywords: wise, contemplative, achiever, determined, stubborn, active

8 Keywords: independent, wise, loving, assertive, confident, dynamic, detached, selfish

9 Keywords: humanitarian, ambitious, responsible, justice-seeking, idealistic, unselfish, driven, opinionated, judgmental

—Michelle Arbeau (www.MichelleArbeau.com) is an internationally known intuitive numerologist, author, inspirational speaker, and radio host. Michelle is the host of "SURVIVING THE SHIFT, a radio show with a focus on practical spirituality, and is the president of Authentic You Productions Inc., a total health/wellness event planning and hosting company. She is currently writing her first book, *The Power of Words: Harness the Vibration of Language & Transform Your Life.*

Can a person's name, turned into a single master number, then be defined by a system of divination? As with palmistry, is it all set in stone, or in numbers, before we are born, or at the moment of birth? And once our parents name us, have they imbued upon us more than just a moniker to respond to when someone calls us? Astrologer/palmist Jagjit Uppal wrote in his introduction to *Cheiro's Numerology and Astrology* of the dilemma free will and destiny play in these systems of fate and fortune. Uppal believed that there is some scope for free will to exist within the "choice and discrimination" we use to lead our lives. Although the events of our lives, including our own births and deaths, are not up to us and we have no choice in them, we could still use the ancient arts to better understand ourselves, and thus possibly "conduct our lives in a more orderly manner."

Still, though, Uppal suggested that the stars and the numbers were pretty fixed in what they "saw." Although some astrologers, *et al.* might suggest that the planets and lines of the hand are more about trends than circumstances, he saw it as a contradiction: "For if we cannot say with certainty what is in store for us in the Future, then there is hardly any need to study the subjects."

Cheiro, born Count Louis Hamon, is often regarded as the most well-known astrologer, palmist, and numerologist of the 20th century. Though his work is steeped in controversy and again accepted only as pseudoscience to mainstream academia, his work has fascinated readers for decades, propounding the ancient view of the influence of the known planets upon the earth and upon humans: "Long before man made his creeds, or civilizations and their laws, the influence of these seven planets had become known on earth. Out of the dark of antiquity their light became law and as far as we can penetrate, even to the very confines of prehistoric days, in all races, in all countries, we find the influence of the seven planets through all and in all."

This is a very extreme belief, that the planets influence everything, and everyone, but one that held high regard for thousands of years, with kings and priests and royalty often keeping a numerologist or astrologer as part of their household or governing body. Many a major decision has been made by some historical figure consulting an astrologer for advice, guidance, and direction.

If one is born under a certain sign, is one destined or fated to a life over which little or no control can be exerted? Are events predicted in the stars signed, sealed, and delivered, or just suggestions of what might happen if a certain course of action and choices is taken? Buddha considered any kind of fortune-telling system to be a "low art" and taught his disciples that there was no such thing as Fate or luck. Instead, everything happened because of a specific cause, leading to an effect, as we discussed in the first chapter. There had to be a definable relationship between the cause (say, being exposed to someone with the flu) and the effect (getting the flu yourself). Fate had little or nothing to do with it.

But some will argue that you were fated to be exposed to the person with the flu to begin with, and your presence in his or her company was predetermined before you were born, as part of a chain of events that, in the end, would make up your destiny. There really is no way for sure to prove either one, either way, but it is intriguing that eastern teachings and wisdom are so infused into all of the divination systems discussed here, including astrology.

iChing

As in the use of the 64 hexagram combinations of the iChing and its corresponding Book of Changes to seek advice and wisdom, the East has shaped the thoughts and beliefs of the world to this very day. The iChing, the standard text of which is said to have originated during the Han Dynasty of approximately 50 BC to 10 AD (although an extant text is said to be at least 5,000 years old), again links to the importance of numbers and number sequences by suggesting that the 64 possible hexagram patterns represent all potential situations and solutions for any life circumstance. There are basically eight trigrams of lines and dots that can make up 64 hexagram combinations, based upon knowledge and observations of the natural world and the interplay of yin and yang dualities, as well as the connectedness of everything in the universe. The various patterns can also act as oracles to tell a person's fate or fortune, which is still today an important part of Chinese culture.

The iChing would be read and analyzed often in relation to Taoist beliefs, and was mainly used to provide interpretation and significance to events, and show the processes of change that were inevitable within the natural world. It could also suggest the right times to act upon something, or take a certain route or life direction. Again, all within the framework of existing Taoist ideas of the interplay of dualities and the constancy of change.

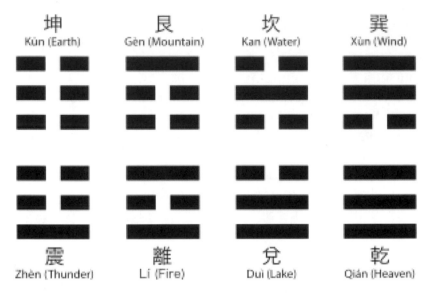

Fig. 3B

The eight trigrams from which 64 hexagram combinations can be created in the iChing.

Tarot and Destiny

To the Europeans, the Tarot was the oracle of choice and is one of the most popular tools for divination used today. The Tarot consists of a pack of 78 cards, originating from the 15th century, that were once used to play games with, quite like our typical deck of cards we all know and love. It wasn't until sometime in the latter part of the 18th century that the cards were looked upon as an occult divination system using hidden symbols and knowledge. The name most likely came from the French *tarau*, one of the many games played with the original deck in France, although in Italy it was referred to as *tarocchi*.

The cards consist of a "major arcane" of 21 trump cards and a Fool card, and a "minor arcane" of the remaining 56 cards, broken down into 10 "pip" cards and four court cards in each of four suits

(14 cards per suit; think our usual suit cards). The use of Tarot in divination is often accredited to a 15th-century book called *The Oracles of Francesco Marcolino da Forli*, and from the 1700s on developed into a more sophisticated form of divination, with individual meanings assigned to each card, as well as to the particular order and layout of the cards chosen for the reading.

In the 18th and 19th centuries, these colorful and often beautifully artistic decks would become the favorite tools of occultists and mystics, due in large part to the publication of *Le Monde Primitif*, a book detailing religious symbolism by Swiss clergyman Antoine Court de Gebelin. Additional texts would expand upon the Tarot as an interpretive system of not only divination, but imparting esoteric wisdom in hidden form. Gebelin in fact claimed the word *tarot* really originated with the Egyptians as *tar* for "royal" and *ro* for "road." Thus, Tarot was the "royal road" to knowledge and enlightenment.

To date, there are hundreds of decks in existence, which again poses the dilemma: If the Tarot is truly a divination system, or an occult storinghouse of hidden knowledge, well, which deck is the one true deck? Much of the original symbolism, if we can even find the original symbolism, has been altered, changed, edited, revamped, and revisited. Thus, the meaning behind the symbols must also change to accommodate the symbol images. Someone getting a reading would again be at the mercy of the reader's own beliefs about the Tarot, the Tarot deck involved, and the interpretation of the symbols on the chosen layout of cards.

Because of the Tarot, dozens, if not hundreds, of other "oracle card decks" have appeared on the market, each promising to show a person's road to knowledge and destiny. Perhaps it has nothing to do with the cards at all, and any deck will do, because in a sense, it's the choices made by the person asking for the reading, and the answers he or she receives from the reader, that are the "fixed destiny" all along. Therefore, would it matter which deck was used and what symbols showed up? Maybe the cards and the person reading the cards give the same fixed interpretation no matter what.

Or, as in other systems of fate and fortune, could the cards be nothing more than whispers of guidance, like our own intuition, suggesting possible solutions and outcomes that we alone have the choice to take or leave when we pay the reader and leave?

Free Will and Tarot

The concept of "free will" is so vast and deep that I cannot possibly cover it within the constraints of one, short article. I am certainly no philosophical expert either, so I shouldn't try to pretend to understand the various nuances and arguments for and against free will, Libertarianism, Determinism, and all the branches of each. Instead, I will attempt to simplify the definition of "free will" as most of us understand it, show the opposing view in simplified terms, then attempt to marry the two in relation to Tarot readings and outcomes.

Why do you choose to do what you do? Choosing what color socks one wears may not be the most earth-shattering decision ever made, yet maybe you chose blue socks because they match your outfit better than white. Choosing to go out to dinner with a prospective date is a bit more complicated. You must factor in first impressions, personal tastes, how you are feeling at the moment, and whether or not you have previous engagements. Compound that with all other factors, including whether or not it would be worth it to break a previous engagement, and a simple yes-or-no decision truly becomes dizzying. However, we must not confuse complexity with choice.

Look back for a moment on your life and think about all the major (or minor) decisions you've made throughout the years. If you had it to do over again, knowing only what you knew then, would you do things any differently? Obviously, hindsight is perfect vision, but based on what you knew back then, would you have made a different decision? The answer, according to those who do not believe in free will, is an obvious "no." You would have still married that jerk of an ex because at the time, you felt it was the right thing to do. You would have still put on the blue socks, not realizing until mid-day that one of them was actually black. You would have done exactly what you did, given the circumstances and information you had at the time were exactly the same.

So, how does this fit in with Tarot? Let's see if we can unravel this knot a bit:

I've been reading Tarot seriously for about a year now. One thing I've discovered to be true is that the cards are never wrong. That doesn't mean that the reader necessarily knows what he or she is talking about, though. It's all in the interpretation. The cards, I've also discovered, tend to give you the reading you need, if the need is great enough. One man asked the cards what he should be when he "grew up." The cards he drew didn't make a lot of sense until, some time later, he came to me with his real question: "Should I stay with my spouse?" Upon reflection, we discovered the first reading gave him the answer and the second reading confirmed it.

In another reading nearly every card was reversed. I had never seen anything like it (and no, I didn't flip the deck. I even double-checked to make sure). So I gave her the reading as if the cards were not inverted, and then explained to her that this could be her life if she chooses to "flip" her situation around. She agreed that her life was a bit "upside-down" at the moment and resolved to "flip" things to change her situation.

In a third example a client asked if his marriage was going to last. The reading didn't give good news on that event, but that didn't stop him from trying. In each of these cases, the cards were quite clear in their messages. Sometimes the cards will say "If you continue along this path, this will take place. But you do have a chance to change it." Other times, the cards tell you that you will get what you desire, but there is a bit of waiting involved. My experience has been

Fig. 3C
Anna Byers and her cards.

that no amount of "free will" or desire can change this, or similar readings. Sometimes, what's in the cards is, well, it's in the cards. Other times, we do have that choice, but it's definitely a case-by-case situation.

Do we have the ability to change our future? Is what the cards tell us our destiny? The answer to those questions, in this author's opinion, is "sometimes." Sometimes, things are meant to be. Other times, we do have the choice and ability to shape our future. Wisdom comes in the ability to differentiate between the two.

No names are given to protect privacy. Genders may or may not be "flipped" for the same reason. If this story sounds familiar to you, it's probably because 99 percent of the readings I do are on one of two questions: love or money.

—Anna Marie Byers is, among many other things, the co-host of the popular radio show "Ghostology with Brian & Anna Marie," which can be found on fateradio.com every Friday night at 10 p.m. Eastern.

I have had several Tarot readings, and sometimes they are so on the mark I am left speechless. Other times they appear so vague, I could just about interpret anything that happens to me in the next year as fitting in with the reading. Maybe Tarot readers, like other readers, are simply tapping into an existing field of information and pulling up what they see. I could learn to do the same, with or without need of cards or stones or even stars or numbers. If I choose certain cards, and they are laid out in order, then read and interpreted in that order, am I choosing right then and there my destiny? Or am I just confirming the one that already exists, except in a manner that seems, at the time, random?

On a Tarot-related website, the topic of destiny came up. One of the respondents suggested seeing the Tarot as a "close friend," someone that knows you through and through, and therefore knows what is best for you and can offer insight and validation to knowledge we may be hiding from ourselves. I found this explanation so perfect. The cards, then, might not be saying you will do this, then do that, then this will happen, so much as they might suggest doing this, and then when this happens you can do that. There is choice, but also a framework of "best suggestions" from which to operate.

For many people, though, the easier way would be for someone to tell them exactly what will happen and when, because it takes away personal responsibility. Choice is hard, because facing the consequences of choices can be hard. If we can blame it all on the "cards we were dealt," then we will feel so much better playing the victim. This, by the way, is one of the favorite psychological arguments against divination systems: that they, if too fixed in their outcomes, allow people to shirk all responsibility for actions and behaviors—even the abhorrent ones.

But nothing gets more blame for all the good, the bad, and the ugly in our worlds than the planets and stars above us. Relationship go into the toilet? Blame it on Mercury retrograde. Found a new job? Could be Jupiter going direct. House burn down? Wow, that moon in Saturn last week was a stone-cold bitch.

Astrology and Destiny

Astrology is the most widely used of all the divination systems. Even those of us who claim we don't buy into it can often be found perusing our Yahoo horoscope or checking the back of the *TV Guide* to see if we will have a good week or a not-so-good one.

The idea that the very second of our birth, and the exact geographic location, can determine the course of our lives is as ancient as our awe and reverence for the cosmos. If destiny truly is the part we play in the grand scheme of things, then the position of the stars and planets at our birth is that which assigns us our role.

There are those who believe that astrology does not suggest rule over a rigid or fixed destiny, but rather provides us with a record of that destiny so that we can decide if we want to play along with the rules, or break them and make a whole new recording. The ancient study of the stars, originating more than 3,000 years before the birth of Christ, posited that what happened in the heavens had some direct and indirect effects upon those on Earth. "As above, so below," said Egyptian sage Hermes.

Astrology has played a critical role in the shaping of cultural and societal traditions and beliefs both in the West and in the East. Though still considered a pseudoscience, one would be hard pressed to find a person who has not checked his or her individual astrological "horoscope" and either been filled with happiness at the thought of a good day, or dread at the thought of a bad one.

And how many people live by the understanding that when Mercury goes retrograde, all hell breaks loose (or at the least, all good comes to a standstill)?

Astrologers run the gamut from those who see what is written in the stars as symbolic and universal, meant to be interpreted as suggestions, possibilities, and probabilities rather than fixed outcomes, to those who see it as gospel truth and suggest we live by what our star charts tell us. As a form of divination, once again, we have to look at the fact that, though we may as humans be influenced by things like sunspots and tidal pulls, there really is no proof that where Jupiter was in relation to the sun on the day of our birth has anything to do with how great, or how lousy, our lives are today.

I had a chart done for me, an extensive 30-page chart, about 20 years ago, by someone who barely knew me. I will say that I was shocked by the accuracies of personality traits, characteristics, and behaviors the reader laid out in the chart. I was also taken aback by some "personal" events that she documented. But there was still a vague sense of openness to the chart, as if I was being given a glimpse of a blueprint that was written, but that I could erase and make over anytime I chose. Many astrologers would agree that the stars and planets are not there to tell us the exact destiny we face, but a suggestion of the best destiny possible based upon certain traits and characteristics we may or may not be aware of.

Eastern astrology speaks of "Daiva" and "Purusakara." Daiva is Fate, destiny, and the influence of divine forces outside the realm of our personal control. Purusakara is our own individual influence and energy and our ability and initiative to overcome or change our fate. Again, a fine blend of the two may be at work behind the "as above, so below" mentality. In the book *Destiny and Human Initiative in the Mahabharata*, author Julian F. Woods discusses the ongoing polemic found in the classic text between fate and free will. The Mahabharata teaches that outside influences certainly do seem to govern the lives of individuals, but Krishna teaches that we can use human initiative to change our lives, and the lives of others, hopefully for the betterment of all. Ultimately, though, the ancient text takes the side of destiny, and that what seems free choice is destiny hiding in disguise.

The same argument takes place here in the West with astrologers struggling to find a balance in their studies of Fate and free will. Astrology, then, has become more of an interpretive system of prediction based upon symbolism, a system that can help someone identify which things in life one can control and which things one cannot. Control implies free will. Lack of control implies Fate. You can control where you have lunch today. You cannot control whether or not it will rain tonight. Other factors are influencing both, but some of those factors can be overcome by will, and others have to be accepted.

Astrologers state that they work within a margin of error, just as local weather people do when they try to predict rain or shine over the coming weekend. As an abstract system that combines mathematics and subjective interpretation, and an ancient belief in the earth mirroring the heavens, we are again left with ambiguity. If a chart reading hits the mark, we take it as destiny. If it doesn't, we choose to ignore it.

One of the bigger factors against using astrology as a means of understanding a fixed life path or destiny is the fact that there are two major schools of thought at work. Vedic astrology is the system used in ancient India. Most of us know of Western astrology. Both are "horoscopic" systems that focus on casting a chart that represents the positioning of celestial entities such as the sun, moon, and planets, and their influences upon events. The main difference between Vedic astrology and the more commonly known Western astrology or Tropical astrology, is that the calculations of the two systems are different. The Western system uses the Western zodiac, which relates the Earth's Tropics to the Sun, whereas the Vedic system uses the Sidereal zodiac (sidereal meaning "of the stars") relating the Earth to the positions of fixed stars. The difference between the two zodiacs typically gives the same person with the same birth information two very different charts, as the Sidereal zodiac is 24 degrees behind the Western zodiac, which is almost an entire Zodiac sign, thus pushing most people's sun, moon, and rising sign into the sign *before* that of their Western positions. Both systems deserve merit, but most astronomers prefer the Sidereal.

This discrepancy caused a huge social network uproar when, on January 13, 2011, media outlets all over the world reported that the earth's wobble was responsible for changing everyone's zodiac signs to the sign before the accepted one! A Minnesota astronomer started the hoopla by confirming that the earth shifts on its axis and throughout the last 3,000 years, those shifts caused a change in the traditionally accepted zodiac signs *and* even went so far as to introduce a new sign, Ophiuchus (November 29th–December 17th), into the mix.

People went crazy, and for days the news, Twitter, and Facebook talked nothing about this, with people whining and moaning about no longer being Virgos, or having to accept being Capricorns. "All this time I thought I was a Leo," one lamented. "I don't want to be a Virgo, I am a Libra and always will be," another cried out! People struggled with this utter threat to their identities, their

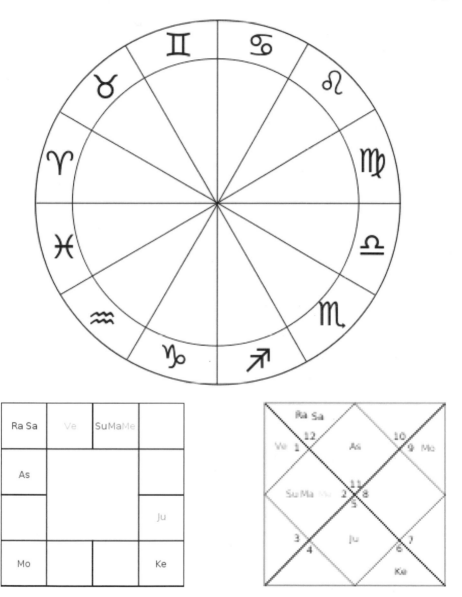

Fig. 3D (Top): Western zodiac; **Fig. 3E (Bottom Left):** Southern Vedic; **Fig. 3F (Bottom Right):** Northern Vedic

characters, and their destinies. "Am I now destined to become arrogant like an Aries?" "Does this mean I have to give up my love of water if I am no longer Pisces?" "Oh, God, I'm an Ophiuchus? What the hell is *that?*" People really got whacked off balance, until the news media got responsible and reported that this sign change was nothing new, and that it was simply Sidereal astrology, or Vedic. Those who followed the Vedic system all along laughed at the display of chaos and anarchy. Tropical astrology was the same as it always was, and Leo stayed Leo, and Virgo stayed Virgo.

How could something like a misinformed news story that went viral totally shake up the human population? Do we not know who we are, and where we are destined to go, without the help of a horoscope? It was, to put it lightly, unnerving.

Western astrologers of today tend to focus more on forecasting trends and developments instead of specific events, whereas Vedic astrologers predict both trends and events. This leaves Western astrology much more open to accusations of fraud and spin, as it is much easier to take a trend or development and interpret it according to the needs of the client, even if there is no immediate connection between the events being discussed. Vedic astrologers, by nature, get a lot more specific, using planetary periods to infer a particular trend, with the transits give the time of significant events. Thus, there can be actual predictions to weigh outcomes against, rather than vague ideas about what may or may not happen when.

There are other systems as well: Egyptian astrology, Persian astrology, Muslim astrology, Hindu astrology, and Chinese astrology. Chinese astrology, which is also practiced in form in Japan, Vietnam, and Korea, uses an entirely different system of sign correspondence than Western astrology. Even in horoscopic astrology, there are different branches, with different focuses, such as natal, mundane, and horary astrology. All come from an origin point at some time around the third millennium BC. All had, at their start, a synonymous relationship with astronomy, and only in more modern times did astronomy break away as the "empirical" science, leaving astrology to pseudoscience. But for all intents and purposes, we focus on the Big Two: Western and Vedic. Most of us know our sun signs and can easily figure out our Vedic sign as well.

Astrological Influence on Human Language

Whether you believe in it or not, astrology has had an influence on our language. For example, *influenza*, from the medieval Latin influential, meaning "influence," was so named because doctors once believed epidemics to be caused by unfavorable planetary and stellar influences. The word *disaster* comes from the Italian disastro, derived from the negative prefix *dis-* and from Latin *aster* ("star"), thus meaning "ill-starred." This suggests that disaster occurs when one's stars are out of sorts. Many of our adjectives come from astrology: *Lunatic* (Luna/Moon), *mercurial* (Mercury), *venereal* (Venus), *martial* (Mars), *jovial* (Jupiter/Jove), and *saturnine* (Saturn) are all old words used to describe personal qualities that resemble or are influenced by the astrological characteristics of the planet. Many are derived from the attributes of the ancient Roman gods they are named after, showing a distinct correlation between mythology and astrology and the use of symbolism to describe character and personality.

And who would want to be "born under a bad sign" or suffer through a "star-crossed" love affair? One might rather thank their "lucky stars" or find their true love "written in the stars."

I was born on October 12th. Therefore, in Vedic astrology, I am a Virgo, although in Western astrology I am a Libra. I have traits and characteristics of both that seem to be accurate, but there are traits of both signs that are not "me" at all. Now, knowing that I am a Virgo in the east, so to speak, I feel like all the years I've lived as a "Libra" may have been a total lie! I am being a little facetious here, but only a little, because having been told since I was a child that I was a Libra, I now have to ask: Did I grow up manifesting Libra qualities because it was my destiny, or because I freely bought into the idea I was a Libra?

Now, when I do check my chart, I check both signs to see what is in store. During the writing of this book, I asked a friend and colleague, Bev Walton-Porter, who is also an astrologer, to do my natal chart. The results were interesting.

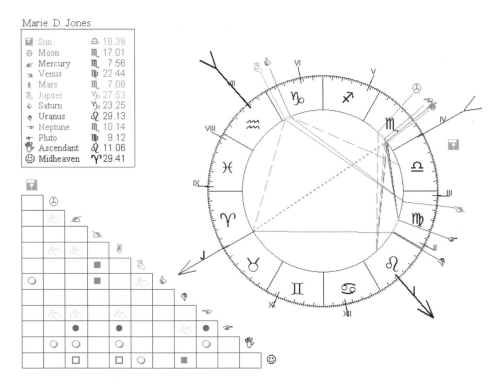

Marie D. Jones

Sun	♎	18.39
Moon	♏	17.01
Mercury	♏	7.56
Venus	♍	22.44
Mars	♏	7.06
Jupiter	♑	27.53
Saturn	♑	23.25
Uranus	♌	29.13
Neptune	♏	10.14
Pluto	♍	9.12
Ascendant	♌	11.06
Midheaven	♈	29.41

Fig. 3G

My natal chart serves as a template of traits, characteristics, and influences that lead to the destiny of my choice.

Bev's reading of my natal chart told me things about my personality, character traits and flaws, and influences of not just the sun and moon, but the other planets as well, all of which can be muted or opposed by other aspects of my chart, and some were on the money, describing me to a T, while others were quite off the mark. Bev explained that the chart is not my destiny; rather it is a "template of influences that could've been manifested in your life, and you've manifested certain ones." Certain influences in my chart, she went on, may be present at my birth time, so the possibility exists for me to manifest these influences—or not: "Just remember the chart is a template with prevailing influences, not all of which will necessarily come to pass. As a human being, you have free will and how you play out/live your life and what influences come into play is up to you in the end."

The choice is mine, allowing me free will within the template my natal chart provides.

"My advice," Bev told me, "is to just be who you are. You've manifested the path of destiny you're on now. I believe your choices, based on free will, opens a certain path of destiny. In other words, who is to say we only have *one* destiny?" By making specific choices, she reminded me, I've selected behaviors and traits that lead me to X destiny. But in another realm, I may have made similar choices, but because of slight alterations, I ended up with Y destiny, or Z destiny, which fits in quite well with the Multiverse Theory discussed in this book. Thus, I was able to look at my chart as a potential blueprint of choices I could make for a destiny that would be the right fit—*for me.*

Ultimately, though, each horoscope we read, or each astrologer we consult, will have a different take on the outcome of our charts, because we simply cannot take the subjective out of the reading. We are then left to decide if we buy into the blueprint we are being presented with, and whether or not we want to act in the manner that will bring us to the fulfillment of that blueprint. Or we can leave the blueprint behind and choose another (yet how do we know that choice itself was not fated?) and follow through with a new series of choices that set off a new series of causes and effects. Just because an astrologer tells me I am a Libra doesn't mean I am all the things being a Libra symbolizes. Libran females are supposed to love fine art and be into high style and beauty. I am a tomboy. I live in jeans, tank tops, and cowboy boots. The finest art I own is what my kid draws for me, and it hangs on my fridge.

And yet, like a typical Libran, I am a justice freak, seek balance and rarely find it, and can't make a decision without first weighing every possible outcome. And I have been told I am one hell of a diplomat. Am I destined to be or not be these things? (And remember that now I have to study up on what it means to be a Virgo as well.) Perhaps. No matter how much I've tried, I am just not into the fine arts and fancy home decorating. I don't want to dress like a model for *Vogue*. I am bored to tears by classic literature, and I will *not* sit still in the presence of unfairness. Can I choose to change? Absolutely. I have free will. But what I find so intriguing is that I feel a strong sense of *not* wanting or needing to change—because this is who I "was meant to be."

Meant to be? According to whom or what? The stars? My birth name? The cards I pick from a beautifully illustrated deck set out before me? An astrologer friend, Beth Rigby, told me: "I believe that the planets affect us at the level of our evolution, meaning, the higher we are in our personal and spiritual growth, the less the planets affect us and we rise above them. However, they are a great starting point. I believe one can grow out of their astrology chart through spiritual growth."

Beth gives the example of an intense Mars Pluto transit as being extremely volatile, but for a highly evolved person who has engaged in spiritual work and growth, it might instead play out as an energized transit allowing them to take action and get things done. To Beth, the positions of the stars and planets at our birth are simply "potential destinies."

More than any other divination method or system, astrology has been studied, researched, and dissected. The failure to show a statistically significant pattern or relationship between astrological predictions and defined outcomes is what keeps the field from ever being considered a true science. And experimental psychologists warn that there are many factors that contribute to a person's perception of the outcome of a reading or chart, some of which are confirmation bias, the habit of recalling good information moreso than bad, and the tendency to "find" events that later fit the predictions, even if there is at most a shaky correlation between the two. One of these factors is called the Forer effect and involves people taking vague description and language, and applying it as specific to themselves, when in fact the descriptions are actually vague enough to apply to a wider population.

The only way to possibly come close to proving the validity of these systems would be to conduct studies throughout decades involving control groups where those being read for knew nothing of the outcome of their readings. For once you tell a person something might happen to him or her, the person's subconscious could run with the idea and create the choices and situations to turn it into a self-fulfilling prophecy. If we truly wanted to know if a person was "destined" to say, become a famous opera singer, despite being tone-deaf since birth, that person would have to have dozens of readings, with dozens of readers of various divination systems, and not one of them would be able to tell the person of his or her musical outcome, thus avoiding tainting the whole experiment. If every single reader, whether he or she be an astrologer, numerologist, Tarot reader, runestone reader, or tea leaf reader, said the same exact things about the person in question, and that person ended up doing exactly what they all claimed he or she would and ended up a famous opera singer, overcoming incredible obstacles, this still would not prove or disprove the existence of destiny. It might prove or disprove the accuracy of a few readers, to say the least, but we still could never be sure that this person's fate of singing opera at the local theatre was set in stone before he or she was born.

This is the dilemma. And yet we still ask the questions, and pursue the answers.

Reading the Rune Stones

The art of divination has been practiced by man for thousands of years—if not longer, for the purpose of seeking spiritual guidance and growth. Although divination itself can be accessed within, one can find focus and clarity by using specific tools, such as the Tarot cards, rune-casting, scrying, and many other methods.

It should be noted that although any divination method provides guidance, as opposed to direct answers as consciousness guides us, it does not take away our responsibility for our own lives. Some

Fig. 3H

find it difficult to conceptualize free will and destiny co-existing together; however, I firmly believe they do. They are not separate things, but rather they work in tandem. Think of our lives as a vast road map. It is pre-written and has many roads that branch off into other directions, which in turn repeat the process. Each road has sign posts along the way that you generally can't see until you travel past it. This map reflects destiny—except that as you can envision, we have many destinies—not just one—from which to choose.

Every day we come across these forks in our path—and we can recognize these by our decisions. From simple things like how we dress for the day to what route we take to get to work; to greater things like what career path one should take, or should one stay in a specific relationship. The decisions that steer us are mainly on a subconscious level, and should we instead be conscious of every decision we make, and how they affect others, we can greatly enhance our own lives. If you live a life in self-service, you can bet karma places potholes in your path until you clear that negative energy. If you live your life in service of others, and in balance, the universe responds likewise.

Free will comes in as our choice of road we decide to take. When we get to a fork in the road, although divination cannot tell us what lies exactly at the end of the road, it can help us read the sign posts that follow the course of it, and therefore allow us to make a more informed decision.

Those drawn to the art of divination tend to find the method that calls to them; this was true for me with runes. The art of casting runes is an ancient form of both communication as well as divination. The more recognized runes today are mainly believed to have been introduced by the upper Nordic regions, where the art quickly spread its way across Europe with variations such as the Ogham script, Anglo-Saxon Friesian, and Elder Futhark—though it should be noted that runes stem across many cultures and time, such as the ancient Sumerians, Chinese, Egyptians, and more.

When a tool of divination calls to you, it instinctually speaks with you, and although it may help to study and research its background, the actual understanding of how to use this tool tends to come to one naturally. For example, when casting runes, one first needs to be in a meditative frame of mind—that is one pushes the ego aside, and allows the energies of consciousness to flow through and speak to him or her. I also find that these energies are enhanced by the elements, be it wind, earth, fire, or water. For example, one can cast via candlelight, or sitting on the ground or by a fountain or stream; though this is relevant to the caster's preference.

The cast is based on a particular subject, which may or may not be known by the person performing the cast. Rather it is focused on by the one being cast for. When runes are laid out their meanings work together to provide spiritual guidance that may read differently were each rune to be translated separately. Ultimately the person who receives the cast can truly decipher its meaning. Runes are also as talismans worn on jewelry. The power of the letter alone can signify and attract that with which it embodies. For example, the rune Gebo stands for love and forgiveness, and thus can help attract this into your life.

—Cheryl Deist

Four

Cosmic Plans, Quantum Possibilities: The Science of Fate and Free Will

"We have more possibilities available in each
moment than we realize."
—Thich Nhat Hanh

"Fate laughs at probabilities."
—E.G. Bulwer-Lytton

"Coincidence is God's way of remaining anonymous."
—Albert Einstein

What does science have to say about destiny and free will? Well, that all depends, quite literally, on how you look at it. Perception and observation indeed play a key role in the quantum world in determining the outcome of a given experiment. It appears there is an Observer Effect that helps direct the actions of particles, even at a distance. Because the quantum world is really nothing but probability and potentiality just waiting to be turned into certainty and fixed position, one could say all of what we call reality is nothing more than the choices we, the observers, make.

But that would not be the whole story. A deterministic universe demands cause and effect. Pure potentiality, or probability, suggests the opposite—that there is no cause or effect, until someone or something makes a choice and then initiates the cause and effect chain, that first cause from which all else is determined like falling dominoes. So, if the quantum world tells us one thing, and the grander world another, what are we to believe? It appears that our universe is a little bit of both....

Scientists once believed that the universe was all about cause and effect, with the Big Bang as First Cause, from which the chain of causality continued to this day. Everything beyond that moment of the Big Bang was determined, based upon the forces and laws inherent in the act itself, which eventually created planets, galaxies, stars, and all the chemicals for life itself. Without the First Cause of the Big Bang, there would not be the proper elements and actions in place for life to ever have occurred.

You can't set up and knock down a row of dominoes without pushing the first one down. It starts with a First Cause, and ends as a result of that cause, with the effect of a line of flattened dominoes on the floor.

The Bang Effect

New research out of the University of Oxford in England proposes that there was not just one Big Bang, but rather a circular chain of Big Bangs that cycled through epochs of endings and beginnings. Theoretical physicist Roger Penrose, along with Vahe

Gurzadyan of the Yerevan Physics Institute in Armenia, proposed a new theory that involves potential Big Bangs, based upon their findings of circular patterns in the microwave background left by the Big Bang. This goes against the standard current idea that only one Big Bang went bang and that inflation then occurred, resulting in our known universe. Instead, these physicists propose a series of "starting guns" and that our own Big Bang was simply the last one to go off.

Even cosmologist David Spergel of Princeton University told *ScienceNews.org* in November 2010 that the "Penrose Model" contradicts the inflationary model and rests on the existence of circular large-scale coherent features in the microwave background. He did, however, state the need for much more detail of the analysis, which Penrose states could involve circles that were generated by collisions between black holes.

Whether this theory proves fact one day matters, because if we want to call the universe deterministic, we have to find First Cause. And if we go looking for First Cause, it may not have been the Big Bang, as we thought it was. In fact, to present the theory of a deterministic universe, we may now have to go way back before the bang to get an answer, if there even is one, because if these massive events occurred in a cyclical "loop," was there even a beginning? Does a circle have a beginning and an end?

Physical Laws

Regardless of when it all began, it did begin, and something had to make a choice to begin it. Since then, the universe we live in is governed by fixed and constant laws of physics that direct motion, gravity, the speed of light, entropy—all of them laws that give the cosmos a destiny, if not a design. We can trust that the sun will always rise in the morning and then set in the evening, and that there is a particular process by which planets, stars, and galaxies are born and even die. We know that day follows night, and seasons change, and the starlight we see is from billions of years ago.

Fixed physical laws, sophisticated and intricate in their complexity, give us the sense that, as Einstein said, God truly doesn't play dice. Everything works like a piece of the massive machine, each piece necessary and perfect in its design and purpose. The Universe does appear to have a destiny that leaves little room for choice. And even if it did, we would then have to argue, who makes the choice to change things on a cosmic scale?

For something to pass as a physical law, it has to be both observable and empirical. Scientists must be able to observe the law at work, and to conclude its fixed nature based upon repeatable experimentation and observation. These laws become the fundamental basis of our scientific knowledge, although they, like anything else, occasionally are challenged and overthrown when we gain new knowledge of our environment through improved technology and observation techniques.

Physical laws are also absolute, stable, and unchanging, and appear to be universal, applying to every part of the known universe (although even this is being challenged by theories that the known laws of the universe don't behave in *all* parts of the universe!). These laws also are complex, yet simple enough to be whittled down to a singular mathematical ratio or equation. Without such laws of nature (which are completely different from natural law!), we would have little understanding of the world we live in, and absolutely no basis for increasing our knowledge, for without a set point to work from, where can you go?

An umbrella term, *physical laws* can include laws of physics, biology, evolution, relativity, and so on, but all appear to reflect mathematical symmetries, ratios, and influences found in the natural world that deal with time, space, and energy. These laws are rarely, if ever, violated (think light speed) and when they are, again it is because of a truly monumental forward thrust toward a new understanding of the world based upon better, faster, and more capable technology. The once-flat world was deemed spherical because observation techniques improved, thus stretching the human mind to do likewise and create a new physical law: The world is not flat at all.

In many cases, when a fixed law is usurped, it is often because of a few minor tweaks in observation. Thus, light speed will no doubt one day be surpassed, yet the speed of light may itself never change. The laws we are most familiar with are (described simply, for this is *not* a tome on physics and laws of nature!) the following:

Gravity

One of the four "fundamental forces" of the universe, along with electromagnetism, and the strong and weak nuclear forces. Gravity is the attracting force between objects possessing mass. Newton's Law of Gravity came to him after observing an apple fall from a tree, and wondering if the same force applied on the moon, for if the apple falls to the ground, why not the moon to the earth? In his masterful work *Philosophiae naturalis principia mathematica, Mathematical Principles of Natural Philosophy*), he wrote that "every particle of matter in the universe attracts every other particle with a force directly proportional to the product of the masses of the particles and inversely proportional to the square of the distance between them."

To put it more simply, we think of gravity as the force that holds everything down—including us.

Light Speed

The speed of light is a physical constant in which light and electromagnetic radiation travels in a vacuum or empty space. This is exactly 186,282 miles per second and is totally independent of the motion of the light source, and of the frame of reference of the observer if inert. Light can travel at a lower speed through various materials, but this is the upper limit of light speed—as of this moment in time. Though light appears to move instantly through space to us, on a cosmic scale the speed is noticeable. In fact, it takes approximately eight minutes and 19 seconds for sunlight to reach us here on planet Earth!

Laws of Motion

Isaac Newton also developed Three Laws of Motion to describe the movement of physical objects and the relationships between acceleration of objects and the total forces acting upon those objects. The First Law states that for the motion of an object to change, a force had to act upon it. This is the Law of Inertia. The Second Law further defines the relationships between mass, force, and acceleration, and the Third Law states that for every action there is an equal and opposite reaction between objects. These three laws were first described in Newton's *Principia* back in 1687.

Newton also took prior observations made by German physicist Johannes Kepler about the laws of planetary motion, and updated them with his own ideas more than 100 years later to describe in mathematical terms the motion of planets.

Laws of Thermodynamics

When it comes to the transfer of energy and heat, or the ability within a system to transfer one form of thermal energy into another form (electrical, and so on), we have four governing laws of fundamental physical quantities of temperature, energy, and entropy, which also describe thermodynamic systems and how heat is transported and converted in thermodynamic processes. Thermodynamics is critical in importance because, in essence, everything that happens is due to the flow of heat from a hotter place to a colder place, and is an exact science that truly explains the way the Universe operates. The problem is, most people equate heat with temperature and miss the importance of thermodynamic properties, which are all about energy—heat energy.

- *The zeroth law of thermodynamics defines empirical temperature based on the principle of thermal equilibrium.*
- *The first law of thermodynamics is also known as the law of conservation of energy and states that the flow of heat is a form of energy transfer.*

··· The second law of thermodynamics is also known as the law of entropy, and states that the entropy of an isolated macroscopic system never decreases.

··· The third law of thermodynamics concerns the entropy of a perfect crystal at absolute zero temperature, and implies that it is impossible to cool a system to exactly absolute zero.

Relativity

Einstein always has to be the troublemaker. In 1905 he introduced to the world his Special Theory of Relativity, followed by his General Theory of Relativity 10 years later, thus undermining many of the fixed ideas of Newton's much-earlier theory of gravitation, showing that Newton's laws broke apart when in the presence of strong gravitational fields (Special Theory), and were thus an approximation, and also proving that Newton's Three Laws of Motion were only approximations that changed when taking velocities approaching light speed into consideration (General Theory).

To keep it simple, the Special Theory of Relativity that proved so groundbreaking and earth-shattering to the world of physics describes the structure of space-time and states that the laws of physics are the same for all observers moving at a constant speed relative to one another, and that the speed of light in a vacuum is the same for all observers. Time did not flow at a fixed rate outside a vacuum, as a moving clock might seem to be ticking at a slower rate than a stationary clock. But in a vacuum, it was always the same, and this theory was valid for all systems that are not accelerating. Matter and energy also became interrelated and gave birth to the famous equation of energy equaling mass times the speed of light squared: **$E=mc2$**. This theory is limited, however, to objects or bodies that move in the absence of a gravitational field.

Ten years later, Einstein figured out how to include gravity into the equation and created his theory of General Relativity, which states that space-time is curved and that matter causes pace to curve (think of dropping a heavy bowling ball onto a stretched out blanket), and gravitation affects the flow of time as well. The most basic element of this theory states that a uniform gravitational field is equal to a uniform acceleration. Think of being in an elevator. A person can't tell the difference between standing on earth with gravity pulling him or her downward and standing in an elevator accelerating upward at the right rate of 32 feet per second squared. The person would feel the same pull of gravity keeping his or her feet on the ground. Time would also be effected by the curvature of space-time in that it may slow down or dilate in reference to gravitation.

Other Physical Laws

There are additional laws that affect the relationships between electrically charged particles, laws of momentum, of fields, of natural selection and evolution and economics (Hicks-Marshall, Hotelling's, Bowley's) and environmental science (although many would argue them as theories), and even laws that govern planetary positions (Titius-Bode), linguistics (Zipf), and the growth of technology (Moore's, Gilder's, Metcalfe's). There are laws governing nuclear forces, electromagnetism, and other cosmic influences. There are laws of mathematics that describe the very laws of the universe we are discussing right here! And of course, there is the most important law of all, Murphy's Law, and we all know that one works on a regular basis!

The interesting thing about all these laws is that they hint of destiny, but only on a cosmic scale, because many of these break down at the quantum level, where choice and free will become more evident. Cosmically, everything seems to have happened just the way it should have for all of the elements to fall into place to allow for the existence of planets, stars, and eventually the gasses and chemicals that made up life. It all seems to be planned, leading many to suggest some sort of Intelligent Design at play.

Ratios of Life

In my book with my coauthor Larry Flaxman, *11:11—The Time Prompt Phenomenon: The Meaning Behind Mysterious Signs, Sequences, and Synchronicities*, we explored in depth the magical and profound nature of numbers. One of our chapters delved into the work of Sir Martin Rees, the Royal Society Research Professor at Cambridge University and Astronomer Royal. His book *Just Six Numbers* posits that there are basically six fundamental numbers that are at the foundation of the entire physical cosmos. He describes these as constant values that define everything from the way atoms are held together to the amount of matter in our universe. Imprinted during the Big Bang, these processes began the chain of cosmic evolution that allowed for the creation of stars and galaxies, energy, matter, and even life itself.

Rees recognized the patterns and regularities in nature that allow various phenomena to be put into general categories and laws. But the most amazing thing about this theory of "just six numbers" is that Rees and many of his colleagues and fellow researchers suggest that these mathematical values are so perfectly and intricately designed, that if any of them were "untuned," or tweaked in any way, shape, or form, the universe as we know it would not exist.

The six fundamental numbers that shape the universe that we wrote about in *11:11* are:

1. Nu—"N," *a critically huge number with the value of 1,000,000 ,000,000,000,000,000,000,000,000,000,000—is a ratio of the strength of electrical forces holding atoms together, divided by the force of gravity (which is 10 to the 37th power) between them. If this number were smaller, even by a few zeros, it has been posted that the lifespan of the universe would be too short for biological evolution to occur. As Rees states, a short-lived universe would mean that no creatures could ever grow larger than insects, with no time for biological evolution to unfold. Thus, a buggy world indeed.*

2. Epsilon—0.007—is another ratio, this time the proportion of energy released when hydrogen fuses into helium. This number defines how firmly atomic nuclei bind together and how all of the atoms on Earth were made. The value of epsilon controls the power from the Sun and how stars transmute hydrogen into all the atoms of the periodic table. Carbon and oxygen are common, and gold and uranium are rare, because of what happens in the stars. Were this number 0.006, or 0.008, Rees states that we could not possibly exist, again suggesting that the most minute tweaks would have resulted in a universe far different than this one.

3. Omega—the cosmic number 1—measures the amount of material in our universe: galaxies, diffuse gas, and "dark matter." Omega refers to the relative importance of gravity and expansion energy in the universe. According to Rees, a universe with too high an Omega level would have collapsed long ago; too low, and no galaxies would have formed. The inflationary theory of the Big Bang says Omega should be 1, but astronomers have yet to measure its exact value. Some scientists point to the finely tuned initial speed of expansion as a hint of Creative Intelligence.

4. Lambda is the force of cosmic antigravity, which was discovered in 1998. This is an extremely small number and appears to control the expansion of the universe; however, it has no effect on scales of less than a billion light years. If Lambda were any larger, its effect would have stopped galaxies and stars from forming and cosmic evolution would have been stifled before it could even begin.

5. $Q = 1/100,000$: The basic seeds for all cosmic structures such as stars, galaxies, and clusters of galaxies were imprinted in the Big Bang itself. The fabric, or texture, of our universe depends on a number that represents the ratio of two fundamental energies.

If Q were smaller, the universe would be inert and without structure; if Q were much larger, the universe would be a violent place where no stars or suns could exist, dominated by giant black holes.

6. Delta—3—the number of spatial dimensions in our world. Rees argues that life can only exist in three dimensions, not two or four (at least in our universe, but not necessarily in others). This number, it seems, has been known for hundreds of years, but is now being viewed in a whole new way, especially in light of superstring theory, which posits that the most fundamental underlying structure are vibrating superstrings that operate in a potentially 10-dimensional "arena."

Here's an example of how this fine-tuning of the universe is so critical, and why it speaks of a sort of "master intelligence" behind it all is this:

If the strong nuclear force constant *was larger*: No hydrogen would form; atomic nuclei for most life-essential elements would be unstable; thus, no life chemistry. *If smaller*: No elements heavier than hydrogen would form: again, no life chemistry.

Also, *if* the gravitational force constant *was larger*: Stars would be too hot and would burn too rapidly and too unevenly for life chemistry. *If smaller*: Stars would be too cool to ignite nuclear fusion; thus, many of the elements needed for life chemistry would never form.

And *if* the electromagnetic force constant *was greater*: Chemical bonding would be disrupted; elements more massive than boron would be unstable to fission. *If lesser*: Chemical bonding would be insufficient for life chemistry.

These tweakings could be ever so slight—in fact, almost imperceptible—yet still result in a drastically different end game, one in which we most likely would not exist. Could this be some evidence of predeterminism? That whatever created the universe knew exactly what to do and in what amounts? That the universe has a meaning, a nature and a fate all its own, decided ahead of time long before we conscious human beings with our power to choose freely came along?

The circumstantial evidence certainly points to some kind of intelligence at hand, or as some of a more metaphysical bent might suggest, a higher consciousness that is self-governing and evolving, thus always creating new life and expansion and growth. Religious people call it God. Information theorists call it "its and bits" of information that increase exponentially, creating more information and more progress and more knowledge. Some even suggest the universe is one giant quantum computer.

Programmed Universe

The idea is that our universe may be a big, gnarly computer of sorts, programmed to unfold in a certain way, taking in new information in the form of particle interactions, and increasing and evolving its own capacity for processing as it goes along. The dynamics of this would lead to a universe that programs itself for constant computational processing, that, as it unfolds, unfolds reality itself.

Professor of mechanical engineering at MIT and author Seth Lloyd takes on this intriguing world of quantum computing (he invented the first one!) in *Programming the Universe: A Quantum Computer Scientist Takes on the Cosmos*. The complex and highly entertaining book delves into the world of "information" and the role it plays in the eventual development and evolution of life, DNA, consciousness, and the entirety of reality itself. First asking the question "why is the world so complex," Lloyd looked to his own field of computation to apply the concepts of information begetting more information, in an exponential growth that could account for the ongoing evolution of both the physical universe, and possible the conscious one as well.

It all comes down to "bits" of information from which "its," or things, arise. In short (because it would take three chapters to truly do justice to Lloyd's work), the idea is that the universe, or even the multiverse, if we are talking about what many scientists believe, could explain a lot of currently inexplicable things (the idea of many, perhaps even an infinite amount of universes, which may or may not have their own laws of physics differing from one to the other), could be like a giant quantum computer that takes in bits and spits out more its, and does so in a looping process where there is always more bits going in, and more its coming out.

What is intriguing, though is that different bits of information play different roles in the universe. All bits register the same *amount* of information, but the "quality and importance of that information varies from bit to bit." The significance of a particular bit could depend on how the information is processed, and how much that bit affects other bits over time. Because the universe is made up entirely of bits, whether we are talking atoms or particles, all of the interactions between bits process the information by altering the affected bits. Thus, throughout time, as Lloyd puts it, "the history of the universe is, in effect, a huge and ongoing quantum computation," which in fact, is computing *itself*. All of this began, of course, when the universe began. Patterns produced then were simple, but as time went on, the processing and computation got more complex as more information was fed back into the computer and reprogrammed into new its from those bits.

Think of your own personal computer. The more you put into it, the more you get out of it. Lloyd writes, "The computational capability of the universe explains one of the great mysteries of nature: how complex systems such as living creatures can arise from fundamentally simple physical laws." Lloyd goes on to say that the physical laws allow us to predict or pre-determine the future, but only as a probability and only on a large scale. Also, the details of the future are unpredictable because the only way to see how the big universal computer is going to process and compute is to wait and see what goes in, and what goes out!

Because we believe the universe will keep on expanding forever, this computation will go on forever as well, and the number of "ops" performed and the number of bits available to be programmed will increase, albeit with some minor caveats involving the increasing density and maximum amount of free energy extracted from the system. But we don't really care because by then we will all be dead.

What we do care about is this: If the universe is indeed a giant computer, who is the Programmer? Or what? It may very well be that the triggering of the Big Bang caused the chain of cause and effect events that made the computer and allowed the process of computation to begin (except...what triggered the Big Bang?), or it may be that there is some Master Programmer behind it all, whether some type of intelligence, or consciousness, we do not yet have the intelligence ourselves to understand. Either way, there is still a distinct destiny or determined outcome to the universe that is based upon the laws that govern and drive it, and the amount of information that computes its ongoing existence.

If there is choice or free will, it is not any of our doing on this grand a scale. But if we go back to the metaphysical argument of a super consciousness, or the religious argument of a God, then that is where the choice and free will comes into play. On the cosmic scale, we have very little say, if any. In future chapters we will see where we do shape our own destiny and choices, but for now, we must give props to something far greater, grander, and just plain bigger than we are as human beings—something that planned this all out in all its glorious intricacy, whether just for the random hell of it, or because it had a reason. Even in randomness there can be a destiny, a plan, built into the playing out of that randomness, however the chips, or cards, or planets may fall. And if the multiverse theory is correct, than our universe is only one of many and our universe just happened, by chance, to look, act, and be the way it is. Pure luck of the Big Bang draw.

Though most scientists will agree, it just doesn't look like randomness or chance at all.

10 Critical Properties

Astrophysicist Bernard Haisch writes in his book *The Purpose Guided Universe: Believing in Einstein, Darwin, and God* about 10 properties that govern the universe, including the ratio of gravitational force to the electric force, the ratio of ordinary matter to dark matter, the just right conditions for the formation of carbon and oxygen, and the average density of matter in the universe. He notes that deviations from these properties, even as small as one part in a million billion, could have changed the entire course of evolution of the universe. "I believe that we live in a purpose-guided Universe governed by the laws of science," he writes, adding that there is no conflict in believing even that a God of some sort, an Intelligent Designer, could have "imagined into existence just the right characteristics that a Universe needed to have in order for life to originate and then to evolve into complex beings, such as you and I."

This "special ensemble conducive to the origin and evolution of life" can be seen as evidence of a destiny for the universe and all life within it. It was thought out, planned, pre-determined, to the exact and minute detail, as nature shows us. We don't have to get into religion here, for God or that Master Planner can be any number of things, or no thing at all, just a Master Mind out there thinking it all into existence. This, of course, implies free will on the part of the Master Minder, as well as a fixed plan for the course of evolution.

In *The Goldilocks Enigma: Why Is the Universe Just Right For Life?* author and internationally acclaimed cosmologist and physicist Paul Davies, who also wrote *The Mind of God,* talks about how our universe appears to be designed for life. He points out that we must make the distinction, though, between design in the laws of physics and design in objects or systems such as biological organisms, because we can actually test the design aspect of living organisms, as in evolutionary theory.

But, Davies does admit that the laws of physics we sense are part of a grand design could possibly also be explained, by the multiverse theory with anthropic selection. Or perhaps it will be explained one day when scientists have their Theory of Everything that is the Holy Grail of knowledge. This, however, would nullify the need for a Grand Designer and possibly open up the universe to chance and randomness, because the observer selection effects would not be present or needed. However, the chances of this seem slim, and Davies and other physicists like to apply Occam's Razor when they can, finding the simplest explanation among the available theories.

Still, Davies suggests that the elements that seem to be perfectly aligned for life suggest that maybe we can look to a different explanation than one that is purely scientific, one in which "life and mind are not just carried along for the ride but play an active role in explaining existence." He suggests a "self-synthesizing universe" or perhaps multiverse, that may "run on an ingenious cosmic code, and if the existence of the code is attributed to a self-consistent, self-explanatory loop, then the state of the universe has to be, at some point in its evolution, equally as ingenious as the laws that underpin it." This speaks of information theory, with information content looping and evolving, yet having possible meaning, as if the universe understood the importance of the laws it is responsible for.

One interesting point Davies makes is science's disdain for teleology, or the belief in final causation. The idea of a universe that is "destined" to create life is clearly teleological in nature, but there may even be a way around that, as in "backward causation" to close the gap. Because teleology anticipates a future state and through time brings about that state, it has been a thorn in the side of scientists who see it conflicting with the laws of physics. "This blatant element of predestination is in sharp contrast with the normal concept of causation in science, in which present events can influence the future but not the past," Davies says. But can the future influence the *present?*

How, Davies asks, could the early universe right after the Big Bang, when the laws of physics themselves were still "in the melting pot," possibly know that billions of years later, life and mind and humanity would emerge?

Enter the opposite world of the cosmic. The quantum. Although some things just don't fly at the grander scale, in the world of the quantum, they might even soar.

The Quantum Enigma

According to Bernard Haisch, in *The Purpose-Guided Universe*, the classical physics of Newtonian laws may have once spoken to a determined, completely pre-ordained reality. This is how things are. These are the confines within which we exist and move and have our being. But along came quantum physics, and all of that got turned on its head. Modern science tends to look at both a mix of deterministic and stochastic explanations for the natural world. Stochasticism is simply the theory that a process is random and non-deterministic, with both elements of predictability and randomness present in the behavior of process in action. If it is all chance, there still may be order behind it. As Haisch writes, mathematical theorist Pierre-Simon Laplace once said, "The word 'chance' then expresses only our ignorance of the causes of the phenomena that we observe to occur and to succeed one another in no apparent order." The Law of Large Numbers even states that there will be an emerging pattern of distribution in random outcomes if you do it enough (say, flip a coin a million times as opposed to 22).

At the level of the quantum, where the behavior of particles reigns supreme, things get a little bit less fixed, and a lot more bizarre. Quantum mechanics is about probability. At the level of the quantum, we are told that particles exist in a suspended state until they are observed and collapsed into one particular (pun intended) outcome. We cannot measure both the momentum and position of a particle, which is also a wave at that point, until we observe it, thus "collapsing the wave function," and give that particle a place, a fixed place.

In the 2007 issue of *Science*, a group of French scientists described an experiment in which they shot photons, or light particles, into an apparatus, and then showed that what the photos did could retroactively change something that had already happened! The photons passed a fork in the apparatus, and had to decide whether to behave like particles or waves as they hit the beam splitter. Later on, long after those very photons had passed the fork, the experimenter could at random switch a second beam splitter on and off. What the experimenter, or observer, decided just then at that moment determined what the particle actually did at the fork—*in the past.*

The observer chose the history of the particle!

Particles have a range of possible, or potential, states, and until an observation occurs, those states remain in superposition, or all happening at once, so to speak. It is hard to say what is more stunning to consider: that an observer can choose the state of a particle simply by observing, or that an observer can *change history* once it's already occurred. Even the great Stephen Hawking has stated that the histories of the universe depend on what is being measured, and that the universe may not have an observer-independent history at all!

If the history of our universe isn't set in stone, perhaps our history as human beings isn't either!

In "Does the Past Exist Yet? Evidence Suggests Your Past Isn't Set In Stone," (*Huffington Post*, August 18, 2010) scientist and theoretician Robert Lanza writes that until the present is determined, how can there be a past? "Part of the past is locked in when you observe things and the 'probability waves collapse.' But there's still uncertainty, for instance, as to what's underneath you feet...." There could be a boulder, or dinosaur fossils, or any number of things beneath you that, if you dug them up and observed or affected them, might actually change their past!

Reality begins and ends with the observer, and light shed on something now will change the path it took then. Constance Hillard, a historian of science, adds that choices we haven't made yet might actually determine which of our childhood friends are still alive, or whether our dog got hit by a car yesterday. She adds, we might even collapse realities that determine whether Noah's Ark sank!

The thing to remember here is that in the quantum world, there is nothing solid. Nothing fixed. Particles act as both particles and wave forms until there is a specific act put upon them, the act of observation, that then stops that wave-ness and makes a particle a fixed and observable particle. Before that happens, anything is possible in that superposition state where all probabilities, potentialities, and possibilities exist. Something has to act upon that super-state to pull out a particular "thing"—sort of like taking some thing out of no thing or, in this case, every thing.

In the cosmic sense, destiny seems set, and there may be choice on the part of whatever banged the Big Bang into happening and programmed the giant universal computer, but for the most part it is all pretty determined. Not one of us, no matter how hard we try, can jump up right now and smack the moon out of the sky with a broom handle. According to the set laws of physics and the natural world, it just is not possible.

Down under, in the quantum world, though, free will and choice seem to be an integral part of whatever evidence of destiny might arise. For example, if an observer chooses outcome A of a photon, then that photon experiences destiny A. Yes, it has a destined outcome or path it will take, but it is entirely dependent upon the choice taken by the observer. And, to make matters even spookier, if observer decides that outcome A is a lousy destiny, then it appears observer can make a new observation and choose outcome B, and get destiny B as a result. It is called "delayed choice," and was made "famous" by physicist John Wheeler's 1978 thought experiment proposing his variation of a double-slit experiment in which the method of detection of a photon can be changed after the photon passes the double slit, and thus delay the choice of whether to detect the path of the particle, or detect its interference with itself. The act of measurement itself determines how the particle passes through the double slits, as a particle or a wave.

Where's my Advil?

Physicist Amit Goswami suggests that Wheeler left something out of his thought experiment: self-reference. In an interview with

Craig Hamilton for the online magazine *What is Enlightenment*, Goswami suggests that an observer's act of "looking" is essential in order to manifest possibility into actuality: "The Universe is supposed to have existed for fifteen billion years, so if it takes consciousness to convert possibility into actuality, then how could the universe be around for so long?" There was no consciousness or sentient observer in that Big Bang fireball to observe it all into actuality. The universe could instead be said to have remained in a state of possibility until there was a "self-referential quantum measurement" that then made manifest the physical reality—including time.

This suggests a purpose to the way the universe has and is evolving, and thus a cosmic destiny, yet one that is based upon a choice of measurement at the quantum level. He calls it "first fruition," and that human beings may not be the "end" of things, but certainly the first, harboring the "possibility of manifest creativity."

Obviously, this brings up the meaning of consciousness as the potential ground state of being, and one that allows choice to exist within what appears to be fixed and governed by other forces we have no power or control over. Goswami had a breakthrough one night where he suddenly saw consciousness as not being a separate and emergent aspect of the brain, but a foundation or ground state that can have "causal efficacy" on its own. This allows for free will and choice to exist at the most elemental of levels. Maybe the universe itself is pure consciousness that evolves in alignment with human consciousness. His idea is backed up by quantum mechanics itself, and as far back as 1932, mathematician John von Neumann was proving that consciousness is a requirement for producing a measurement result in a quantum experiment. So, if consciousness is behind the quantum, it might also be behind the cosmic. Behind everything.

It might be reality itself.

The quantum level allows for the most bizarre behavior of particles, and changes the entire way we look at reality, for even what we deem solid is not. Reality is up in the air, ever in a state of probability and superposition until a choice is made to "collapse" it into a fixed, measureable, manifest form. Particles exist in a state of virtual reality, amid a sea of quantum foam, popping into and out of existence. Although the idea of the observer effect speaks of choice (maybe even consciousness behind that choice!), the quantum world appears to also allow for chance—pure chance—because of the possibilities of various outcomes and alternative histories that are based upon what happens to be observed at any given time. There is quite a bit of uncertainty down at the quantum level, as stated in the Heisenberg Uncertainty Principle of 1927, stating that the more precisely the position of a particle is determined, the less precisely the momentum is known in this instant, and vice versa. Add to that the Copenhagen Interpretation, written by Werner Heisenberg and Niels Bohr, which states that the wave function of the unobserved object is a mixture of both wave and particle, until the experimenter chooses what to observe in a given experiment, thereby collapsing the wave function and fixing a particle into place.

Interestingly, many modern cosmologists have rejected the Copenhagen Interpretation in favor of the multiverse theory, which describes an infinite number of universes that are in fact branches of the quantum state. In other words, the Big Bang was one of an infinite number of beginnings of universes, many with life, many without, all of them branches of the quantum tree.

These fundamental concepts speak of the undivided wholeness that is the quantum reality, even all its realities. Everything is real all at once, yet nothing is real all at once—until the conscious act of observation changes the picture. Einstein was a champion of objective reality independent of what we can observe, yet Werner Heisenberg believed that reality is what can be observed and that different observations would lead to different realities, depending upon the observer. Nothing existed outside of the consciousness of the observer, and what did exist did so because of the choice of the observer to observe it!

In other words, Einstein believed the sun existed regardless of our observing it. Heisenberg felt the sun existed only because of our observing it. Maybe, just maybe, the truth is somewhere in between: that there are aspects of reality that are fixed, and aspects that we create by pure will and intention?

Can one imagine more choice than the opportunity to decide what will be observed and made manifest in the physical sense? Because chance and determinism both suggest one fixed future, the possibilities available in the quantum world shake up the idea that there can be only one choice to choose from! If we are picking various future potentialities out of a literal quantum soup, like macaroni letters we can choose which words to spell out in our dish, then how can we say there is a fixed destiny at work? Are we not, through the act of conscious observation, choosing? How can there be both chance and choice?

Not a Chance!

Chance therefore cannot exist, because we are making it all happen to begin with. Chance implies one randomly chosen future only, the one that is selected by forces outside our control (destiny). Chance takes away choice. Even in a reality with fixed, predetermined aspects, we still believe we have choice. So how much of it is chance and how much choice? How much was determined a long, long time ago by a First Cause we still cannot even identify, and how much is just the outcome of our choice in the present moment?

Chance then may be destiny disguised. We don't see that First Cause that lies behind the random outcome, but just because we don't see it does not mean it isn't there. Think of Carl Jung's description of synchronicity as observing the effects of two unrelated events with a common cause that occurs on an implicate or invisible level. It looks like coincidence, chance, randomness, yet has a hidden order that is valid and real. We only see the two events, or effects. We don't see the cause behind them, so it looks spooky and we say "Wow, what a coincidence!" Chance implies a fixed outcome that we cannot predict, but a fixed one nonetheless. It cannot cause our actions, behaviors, or choices, and therefore we are not responsible for chance events—or are we? We must take this hidden or implicate order of reality into account when we discuss chance or fate or destiny versus choice and pure free will, because so much of the cause may occur here!

Remember: There is order even in the most chaotic of things. There is the hidden, implicate cause to every effect, even if we don't see it with our own two eyes. Reality is like a web, everything connected to every other thing, but not on a level we are consciously aware of. Max Planck, the father of the quantum mechanics, wrote in *The Universe in Light of Modern Physic* that there are realities that exist apart from what our senses can perceive. In those realities, all we consider to be fate, chance, luck, and destiny may indeed have their origin.

We may never truly be able to grasp how much of our world is destined to be the way it is, and how much we choose as we go along, but we can with almost 100-percent certainty say that it all has an initial cause, and until we go all the way back into that very first moment of existence, if there even was one, we won't know what or who drove that First Cause. Think about your own existence. You could easily say that your parents chose to bring you into the world, but you were thought out and planned long before that, as if a part of a massive chain of destiny that goes all the way back to First Cause. Your parents had to be born in order for you to be born. Their parents had to meet, fall in love, and give birth to your parents, and so on and so on. How far back do you go? Apparently, if you want to get incredibly anal about it, all the way back to First Cause! For anything to exist *now*, for any event to take place anywhere in the universe *now*, there is a chain of events that reach far back into time that had to have happened just the way they did in order for *now* to be *now!*

Mind-blowing, indeed. Our destiny was destined a long, long time ago, when something made that first choice that became First Cause. And this is the same for anything that has ever or will ever exist. For many ancient philosophers and spiritual thinkers, that First Cause is *causa sui*, or self-caused cause, oft associated with the miraculous and divine. Regardless, how could it be possible that anything existed without a beginning? And yet, what was before the beginning?

Without a firm grasp of that answer, we are left adrift between chance and its unpredictable, yet fixed outcome that is intrinsically built into the specific chance itself, and choice, where we get to decide all by ourselves both cause and outcome.

Science, both in the cosmic and quantum sense, points to both at work. Clearly there are rules and laws that work at keeping it all functioning the way it has to for life to be supported, and for the expansion and evolution of life as well as the universe itself. As stated earlier, day follows night, and planets orbit the sun, and black holes swallow up everything in their path, and galaxies form, and stars go supernova, and people are born and die. It all happens outside of our control, does it not? And yet, we also see evidence in quantum experimentation of the sheer power of conscious observation, even intention, as we will see in a later chapter, to shape the outcome of our present, our future, and even our past.

There is enough determinism in the universe to make us believe that there is a cosmic destiny afoot. And there is enough potentiality in the quantum world to make us believe we have something to do with the outcome of that destiny. What a fine line we walk between both.

And when it comes to life itself, especially human life, it gets even more interesting. The greatest question about destiny and free will applies not to the physical stage we play out our lives upon, but the role players themselves: us. The world, in all its cosmic and quantum glory may be a balance of both the fixed and the free, but it might also be nothing more than a backdrop for the real action—the real battle.

That battle occurs where the wild things roam.

Five

Stamped for Approval: Destiny and Choice in Genetics, Evolution, and Nature

"I yam what I yam."
—Popeye

"Genetics is about how information is stored and transmitted between generations."
—John M. Smith

"Already at the origin of the species man was equal to what he was destined to become."
—Jean Rostand

Sigmund Freud once said, "Anatomy is destiny." I was born with brown eyes and auburn/brown hair. I got them from my parents, from their genes, which they combined and passed on to me. Throughout my life, I could have chosen to dye my hair blonde, blue, or black, and I often did, or buy contact lenses that would change my brown eyes to blue. That would be my choice, but never my genetic destiny. Nothing would ever change the fact that the "real me" was a brown-eyed brunette.

Genetics are the destiny of humanity. How we look is determined for us before birth, because the chain of influence goes back generations and generations before us. Nowhere is the mark of destiny more obvious than our DNA, which carries within it the information of past ancestors—how tall they were, the color of their hair and their eyes, and the shapes of their faces. We the people are planned out ahead of time, with genetics our designer, like a Master Baker planning out gingerbread men and women for a big holiday soiree.

DNA and Destiny

When it comes to what we look like, we turn to our genes as a blueprint. Children tend to resemble their parents, inheriting certain genes that will ascribe them with eye color, height, and so on. Even a person's gender is genetically determined. We can chalk it up to DNA, or deoxyribonucleic acid, the nucleic acid containing the genetic instructions for development and functioning of all known living organisms.

Genetics 101

DNA is made of nucleotides, two long polymers of simple units or strands, which look like a spiral ladder and run in opposite directions to each other. Attached to each sugar is one of four types of molecules called bases. Encoded DNA information is found in the sequences of these bases, and is read using the genetic code, which specifies the sequence of the amino acids within proteins. Stretches of DNA are copied into related nucleic acid, RNA, in a process called transcription.

Ribonucleic acid (RNA) is one of the three major macromolecules (along with DNA and proteins) that are essential for all known forms of life. Both DNA and RNA are made up of a long chain of components called nucleotides. Each nucleotide consists of a nucleobase, a ribose sugar, and a phosphate group. The sequence of nucleotides allows RNA to encode genetic information.

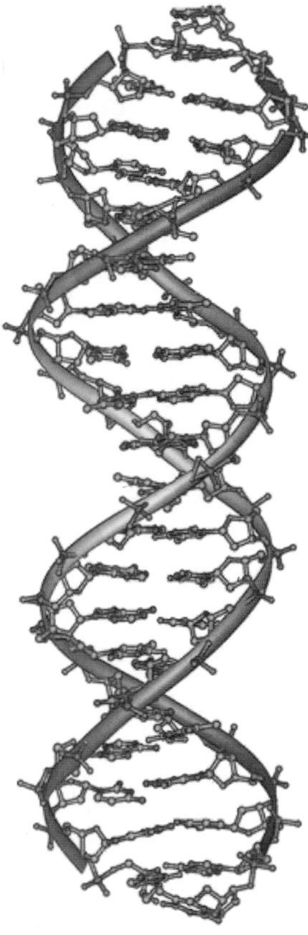

DNA molecules store information and serve as a set of blueprints, or code, for life, because our DNA contains information to build the components of cells, such as proteins and RNA molecules. DNA segments that carry this genetic information are called genes. Genes come in pairs, do not blend, and can be turned on and off. Genes can be exchanged between species, as we've all seen in recent attempts to cross different types of animals. All mutations occur within the genetic information, and different genes are active in different kinds of cells.

Figure 5A

A spiral strand of DNA, or Destiny

Inside each cell, DNA is organized into long structures called chromosomes. Chromosomes carry genes and specialized chromosomes determine gender. These chromosomes are duplicated before cells divide, in a process called DNA replication. Most organisms store DNA inside the cell nucleus and some of their DNA in organelles, such as mitochondria or chloroplasts. Within the chromosomes, chromatin proteins such as histones compact and organize DNA. These compact structures guide the interactions between DNA and other proteins, helping control which parts of the DNA are transcribed. Humans have 23 pairs of chromosomes, for a total of 46. One pair determines sex, and the other 22 pairs, which determine the rest of the body's physical makeup, are autosomal.

An entire set of genes is called a genome, and DNA is only a part of our growing involvement in trying to map the genomes of species of plants and animals, including us humans, and seeing up close and personal what these blueprints are like. The Human Genome Project was completed in 2003, and identified all human genes within DNA. The Human Genome, by the way, is about 3 billion pairs long. That information is now stored in a database, and the Human Genome Project is currently completing the genomes of various plants and living things in a quest to understand the complexity of the structure of life.

What is most fascinating about genes and DNA and genetics is that it speaks of a master plan by which the human body and all living things were formulated and designed.

Does this mean we were pre-determined before birth? Yes, it does, because we inherit genetic information from our parents, just as they inherited genetic information from their parents, and so on and so on. Our entire physicality comes from genetic information that we inherit at conception when the egg and the sperm meet for the first time, securing the actual blueprint from which we will be designed. This also applies on the larger, evolutionary scale.

Homology and Analogy

Traits and characteristics can be inherited in two ways. We can have similarities with, say, our parents or siblings, due to inheritance. These biological similarities are traits that are inherited by two different organisms from a common ancestor. I share brown eyes with my parents and siblings, because we are all related. These traits fall under *homology*, and can include anything from eye color to tooth shape to the shape of a beak, if you happen to be a bird. These are also referred to as inherited traits, and may sometimes skip a generation or two before showing up. The exception would be genetic mutations, which throw a wrench into the works all their own.

We also have similarities because of convergent evolution and not from a common ancestor. This is called *analogy*, and includes acquired traits we might share with others in the form of abilities and skills that are not genetically inherited. For example, this type of trait might include behaviors that help a particular organism survive in its environment, which can be passed on to future generations. Think of a trait like larger leg muscle size in a gazelle from excessive running from predators, which is because of survival necessity and not because of genetic information passed down from parental organisms. If gazelles were not hunted, they would not have a need to adapt to such a hostile environment through time—one that requires extra speed and leg strength, and stamina.

Useful traits are also purposely bred into domestic plants and animals, such as larger crops and bigger pigs for slaughter, which is often part of a very controlled mating process. In 1865, Augustinian monk and scientist Gregor Johann Mendel began to work with pea plants, showing that the inheritance of traits followed particular laws, which were later named after him. He began his work by looking at parents of a known genetic background, then he created a baseline against which he compared patterns of inheritance in the resulting offspring. He counted the number of offspring that showed various traits within each successive generation. Mendel discovered that individual traits are determined by discrete factors that are inherited from parents. These discrete factors would later be known as genes, and Mendel's work would be instrumental in the turning of agricultural cross-breeding into a real science with his experimentation on plant hybridization. His work laid the foundation for the future science of genetics, and he is now considered the father of genetics.

Today, we are cracking the genetic codes for wild strawberries and certain types of cacao used to make fine chocolate, with the hopes of being able to use the genetic information to improve crops, tolerate heat and cold better, increase shelf life, improve taste and avoid pests. While many people cringe at the thought of genetic tampering, it is being made possible by our understanding of the code by which each species of plant or animal is created. The genome sequence is the destiny of that species, the blueprint of that which, long ago, designed it—or by which evolution and adaptation reshaped it.

Genetic Destiny

This book does not dive into the ethics behind genetic engineering of food sources, as that is not its purpose. Instead, we need to look at how even the most intricate and complex coding of a species can indeed be tampered with or altered, once you know the actual code. Thus, if we have a "genetic destiny" we can also, once we know the blueprint, make changes to it to improve our health, longevity, and even appearance.

Homologies and analogies are wonderful examples of the blending of genetic destiny with evolutionary necessity, or choice. The traits we are stuck with because of common ancestors are not by choice, but those we adapt out of the need to survive are purely by choice. So, a child will look like her parents (unless, of course, it's one of those Jerry Springer "mama's baby, papa's maybe" situations!) but that baby could have traits that are uniquely acquired once she is all grown up that were not genetically inherited at conception.

When it comes to our physical bodies, though, destiny wins. Chromosomal damage and mutations can of course offset intended genetic information from being passed along to offspring, and even something like plastic surgery can change the physical human appearance. But the mutations are anomalies, and the plastic surgery is simply a cover-up of sorts, and not a choice of literally changing one's pre-existing DNA. If you have brown eyes by birth, but want blue ones, you can buy blue contact lenses. But that won't change your actual DNA. If you have small breasts and want bigger ones—well, you know the routine, but again, the genetic coding inside of you remains intact, and your offspring will not inherit the new breasts, no matter how much they cost you.

We have choices about how we can look, but in general we cannot change our basic blueprint. Technology and medical advances can give us a hand if we were born without one, make us hear again with implants or even surgical repair, and determine in advance how predisposed we are to certain cancers. We already have genetic pre-natal screening, giving rise to the question of if and when we will be able to correct the mutations discovered. Right now, what is in our DNA stays in our DNA, until we begin the process of altering the actual genomic structure, changing our chromosomes and shifting genetic information in laboratories, moving this protein here and that one there, creating superhumans who are disease free and can live forever—all the stuff of science fiction but right now being researched in universities all over the world. In fact, in a February 2008 report for the Texas Medical Center, reporter Ronda Wendler quotes Francis Collins, PhD, head of the National Human Genome Research Institute, as saying "With the rapid pace of genetic discovery, there's something serious at stake here as we contemplate our future. By identifying genes associated with diseases, we have not only the chance to heal, but also the opportunity to harm. New opportunities for trouble are arising every day." Collins also emphasized that human beings share 99.9 percent of the same DNA. After the sequencing of the human genome in 2003, he admits that the focus has now shifted to the one-10th of 1 percent that makes us all different. This will allow for a future of medicine that moves away from the one-size-fits-all approach to a more unique and individual treatment that matches a person's genetic profile.

Still, the potential for harm remains, as experiments over the last few decades with cloning have shown. It doesn't always make a better machine, especially if that machine is a living thing.

As for superhuman beings courtesy of genetic altering, one potential advocate might actually be the father of DNA research himself, James Watson, the American molecular biologist, geneticist, and zoologist who co-discovered the structure of DNA with Francis Crick, in 1953. Watson was reported by *Salon.com* back in 2000 as saying that a ban on genetic tampering would be disastrous. He said at a 1998 UCLA conference that people would need the guts to try germline therapy, which tampers with the sperm and egg cells to genetically alter not just the individual in question, but future generations as well, even if the end results were not yet known. He even asked at the 1998 UCLA Conference on Genetic Engineering, "...if we could make better human beings by knowing how to add genes (from plants or animals), why shouldn't we do it? What's wrong with it?"

That was more than 10 years ago, and no doubt we are on the verge of making a better human, something that causes tremendous chaos for religious and ethics groups alike.

There are two types of gene therapy being researched widely in the attempt to build a better human.

Germ Line Gene Therapy

Germ cells (that is, sperm or eggs) are modified by the introduction of functional genes, which are integrated into their genomes. Therefore, the change due to therapy would be heritable and would be passed on to later generations. This new approach, theoretically, should be highly effective in counteracting genetic disorders and hereditary diseases. However, many jurisdictions prohibit this for application in human beings, at least for the present, for a variety of technical and ethical reasons.

Somatic Gene Therapy

In somatic gene therapy, the therapeutic genes are transferred into the somatic cells of a patient. Any modifications and effects will be restricted to the individual patient only, and will not be inherited by the patient's offspring or later generations.

Some successes in the last 12 years include:

··· In 2003 a University of California, Los Angeles research team inserted genes into the brain using li-
posomes coated in a polymer called polyethylene
glycol. The transfer of genes into the brain is a significant achievement because viral vectors are too big to
get across the blood-brain barrier. This method has
potential for treating Parkinson's disease.

··· Scientists at the National Institutes of Health
(Bethesda, Maryland) successfully treated met-
astatic melanoma in two patients using killer T
cells genetically retargeted to attack the cancer
cells in 2003. This study constitutes one of the
first demonstrations that gene therapy can be effective in treating cancer.

··· In March 2006 an international group of scientists
announced the successful use of gene therapy to
treat two adult patients for a disease affecting myeloid cells. The study, published in Nature Medicine, is believed to be the first to show that gene
therapy can cure diseases of the myeloid system.

··· In May 2006 a team of scientists led by Dr. Luigi
Naldini and Dr. Brian Brown from the San Raf-
faele Telethon Institute for Gene Therapy (HSR-
TIGET) in Milan, Italy, reported a breakthrough
for gene therapy in which they developed a way
to prevent the immune system from rejecting a
newly delivered gene.

··· In November 2006 Preston Nix from the University of Pennsylvania School of Medicine reported
on VRX496, a gene-based immunotherapy for

the treatment of human immunodeficiency virus (HIV) that uses a lentiviral vector for delivery of an antisense gene against the HIV envelope.

··· On May 1, 2007, Moorfields Eye Hospital and University College London's Institute of Ophthalmology announced the world's first gene therapy trial for inherited retinal disease. The first operation was carried out on a 23 year-old British male, Robert Johnson, in early 2007.

··· In September 2009, the journal *Nature* reported that researchers at the University of Washington and the University of Florida were able to give trichromatic vision to squirrel monkeys using gene therapy, a hopeful precursor to a treatment for color blindness in humans.

··· In November 2009, the journal *Science* reported that researchers succeeded at halting a fatal brain disease, adrenoleukodystrophy, using a vector derived from HIV to deliver the gene for the missing enzyme.

To us humans, the only thing more important than being able to master and control our outer world is to master and control our inner world. Sometimes genetic tampering can save the lives of others, as in the case of "saviour siblings," which involves making close genetic selections at the embryonic stage to insure a baby is born genetically matching a sick sibling. On February 7, 2011, French doctors announced successfully creating a savior sibling that was a close genetic match to a sibling suffering from beta thalassemia, which produces an abnormal form of hemoglobin. The French Associated Press reported that the baby was born at the Antoine Beclere Hospital in a suburb of Paris, and was conceived via in vitro fertilization. The child's embryo had been genetically selected so that he did not carry the fatal inherited disorder, and he was also a close-enough match for umbilical cord blood stem cells.

This was not the first savior sibling; that title goes to American-born Adam Nash in 2000. In this case, the tampering of one person's genetic makeup allowed for another to live and have a destiny of his or her own, but in general, when it comes to altering our own genes, most people are not willing to go that far to change their genetic destiny. Instead, they do the best with what they were given, let go of the things they cannot change, like how tall they are or the shape of their heads, and attempt to change the things they can change, like behavior.

Nature vs. Nurture

When it comes to our physical makeup, we know where we got it all: parental genes. The intermingling of their DNA to create a whole new combination in the form of us. But when it comes to how we humans behave and act, it's a whole new ballgame. Heredity and environment play the two main roles in how we humans develop behavioral traits. Just as the roles of destiny and free will have been debated throughout the years, the roles of nature and nurture have as well, and scientists often take one side or the other. Nature (nativism, innatism) claims that we are predisposed genetically to certain traits, preferences, and behaviors, including those labeled "animal instinct." These are our innate qualities. Nurture (empiricism, behaviorism) believes that we think and behave in ways that we are conditioned and taught to do, perhaps by parents, peers, society, and even the media, and that personal experiences determine physical and behavioral traits in each individual. In fact, both may be right (kind of seeing a pattern here yet, folks?), as we may indeed both have inborn traits and abilities given to us by nature, and genetic tendencies that are molded and shaped according to our maturation in our environment. I may be born with dark hair, but I may have a genetic tendency to lose a lot of hair due to stress and thus make changes in my lifestyle to avoid doing that. I may be born with a wide jawline, but my love for good books may have been a trait I learned from two parents who loved to read and weekly trips to a local library that instilled in me a hunger for books all my own.

When it comes to human behavior, intelligence, emotional maturity, preferences, and overall personality, we have yet to identify a gene that controls that part of our humanity. Scientists seek a genetic component to everything from sexual orientation to whether or not we are capable of murder. But how much of our behavior, even our intelligence, comes from our social conditioning and environment, regardless of what our genes might desire for us? Imagine two flowers of the same species, but each planted in different quality soil. Clearly they will both look the same in general, but the one grown in the better soil with thrive and perhaps even bloom bigger, just as two sisters might look the same, and even act the same, but in some aspects behave differently according to their selected environments.

Perhaps genes provide us with, again, a behavioral blueprint of traits, dispositions, and general patterns that make us unique, but with enough flexibility to account for our environment and the choices we must make within that environment. A child can be born blind, yet because of a loving environment become just as successful as a sighted person. The things that affect us on the nurture end can include not just the usual suspects of parents and peers, but also the weather, the foods we are exposed to, the schools we go to, the friends we attract, and even the clothes we wear. All serve to create a unique individual who may have baselines for behavior, but the full arena of life to either choose those baselines or choose differently.

Numerous studies with twins, both identical and fraternal, have time and again shown that common interests are often maintained between the twins, regardless of how closely they live to one another, yet differences could also occur in areas of political and religious beliefs, work ethic, and even health, all because of where they chose to live. Whereas two twins might share a love of Mozart and Italian food from birth, they might also end up at the extreme ends of the political spectrum because one moved to a red state and one to a blue, and those outside influences proved to help mold their own beliefs.

It might, though, depend on how sensitive we are to outside influences. Nature gives us the baseline, but when it comes to nurture, we might be blindly and involuntarily taking on influences that not only go against our baseline, but that we don't even know we are taking on!

On Auto-Pilot

Behavior may be more about programming and memory patterns than actual choice, though. What we tend to perceive as our reality might in fact be, as some researchers have suggested, up to 90 percent stored memory, which loops and loops, and causes the same reactions and behavioral patterns over and over again. In an article titled "The Small Self: How Your Identity Constrains You," *Huffington Post* writer Mark Eckhardt points to the work of neuroscientists with "invariant representations," which form the model of perception the brain uses to create our reality. He quotes author Jeff Hawkins, the co-founder of Palm and Handspring, who wrote *On Intelligence* along with *New York Times* science correspondent Sandra Blakeslee, as saying "The brain uses vast amounts of energy to create a model of the world. Everything you know and have learned in stored in this model. The brain uses this memory-based model to make continuous predictions of future events." Hawkins focuses on the role of the cortex in the brain in determining intelligence and as a machine to make predictions for temporal sensory patterns that are based on past memory patterns.

Therefore, we are less free with our will than we think, if this past programming is driving the choices and actions we make in the future. Eckhardt likens this so the "small self" of Zen, which constrains us from responding freely and authentically to what is happening outside of us. Rather, we function off of the "activation of stored memory" and not free will. We are living on auto pilot, rarely rising above the small self enough to really think, behave, and react in fresh, new ways that are appropriate to the experience, rather than habit of memory.

In some ways, this is similar to how and why we often notice particular things and deem them fated. For example, we go into a bookstore and see a particular book titled *The Black Swan*, then two hours later, see the same title on a wine label, and then later that day a friend e-mails about the same book we saw earlier, which happened to this author one day. I thought it synchronistic, but there is a part of the brain that is primed to see or notice something new over and over again. The RAS, or Reticulation Activation System, works by seeing a word or image, then scanning the environment for more examples of that word or image, so that when it locks in on one, we think it a great coincidence. Fate. Destiny. We suddenly see that word or image everywhere—on bus bench ads, the sides of trucks, billboards—and we wonder how we never noticed it before. It is simply because the RAS was not activated or primed yet to notice it.

Nature and Nurture

Genetic destiny often means inheriting diseases and illnesses of previous generations, and some diseases, such as Huntington's, are 100 percent genetic, meaning that if you carry the gene for it, you will develop it. Cancers, on the other hand, are often a mixture of inherited genes, exposure to carcinogens in the environment, and even hormone imbalances, and the exposures can be limited by choice. Food, exercise, clean air and water, and even stress reduction are often a large part of how disease develops, if it does at all, but there may also be help within the genes themselves. One day soon, we might even have direct-to-consumer tests that we can buy at the local drug store and test ourselves for various cancers, diabetes, and other debilitating illnesses.

According to Gretchen Voss, in "What's Lurking in Your DNA," for the October 2010 issue of *Women's Health*, DNA research is moving at breakneck speed, and we now have approximately 150 genetic variants that could increase our longevity, but when it comes to testing for potential genetic risks, current DTC (direct-to-consumer) tests leave much to be desired. The goal is to one day perfect the tests, which as of now can be harmful if misread, misinterpreted, or just plain the result of a poorly standardized industry that might end up terrifying more people than it helps.

Even knowing you carry one of the three BRCA mutations for breast or ovarian cancer, or the LRRK2 gene for Parkinson's, doesn't guarantee that disease will one day take your life. Knowing it is a possibility, though, might drive you to make better choices when it comes to diet and lifestyle, perhaps lessening the impact of genetic destiny. Getting more exercise is a big part of that improved lifestyle, and, ironically, there are nearly 40 different gene patterns that can predict your exercise and fitness potential. Researchers suggest that genetics can account for 62 percent of differences in exercise behavior, and genetic screening might one day be a part of developing individual fitness routines, according to genetic epidemiologist Evadnie Rampersaud of the University of Miami. It would be like having a genetic trainer!

According to *Women's Health* magazine, the 62 percent of exercise-related genetics include how hard exercise feels, the maximum oxygen uptake during aerobic activity, and how exercise will improve blood pressure and cholesterol levels. The other 38 percent are factors that come by choice, such as personal motivation and goals, having active friends and family members, and living in a place with plenty of sidewalks for walking and jogging.

Again, even when it comes to our health, our bodies are a mixture of destiny and choice, via our genetic makeup and the quality of choices we make each day.

Apples and Oranges

When it comes to fruit, apples and oranges are the same: They are both fruit. They both grow on trees. They are both nutritious. But try to compare an apple to an orange and you find little more to go on except the aforementioned. Oh, and maybe that they are both rounded in shape. "Nature versus nurture" operates in much the same way, with similarities and differences ultimately making up each individual. Geneticists have identified many single-gene-locus traits, but when it comes to more complex traits, genes alone might not account for them because some of those genetic traits might be influenced by environmental properties. And, the percentage of which a trait is genetic or environmentally influenced will depend upon the genes and the environment themselves.

Even when it comes to intelligence, there seems to be a blend of genetic and environmental influences that work together to form a personality. Working together in concert, genes and environment can contribute to intelligence levels when it comes to language, communication, and even political beliefs, all of which are thought to be partially inheritable. One person might be genetically disposed to liberal beliefs, grow up in a very conservative environment, and still end up a liberal. Much of this is determined by what goes on in the home, society, and culture of an individual.

One of the most studied inheritable traits is personality. Observations using twins and biological siblings have shown that identical twins who grow up in different environments are more similar in personality than two random strangers, and identical twins are more similar in turn than fraternal twins. Biological siblings are more similar than adoptive siblings. But the similarities and differences in personalities are also influenced by home and family size, which are called shared, as opposed to non-shared environmental influences such as pre-natal development. Shared influences are the lives we are born into, and the families we grow up with and experience life with. These influences mold and shape us into who we become as adults, but non-shared influences determine aspects of our personality that we are born with, not into. A child born with fetal alcohol syndrome may not share many of the same personality traits with his or her siblings, because of the effects of the non-shared syndrome.

Emotions also may have a genetic link, and not be entirely about how one was raised or what he or she believes in. Research has long suggested a gene associated with violence, and according to geneticist James Watson, in an interview for the July 2003 *Discover* magazine, that gene can exist in two forms: the gene where one expresses a lot of the enzyme, and the gene where one expresses very little. Watson refers to a study of abused children and the presence of a particular enzyme that correlated directly with whether or not the child got into trouble with the law at an older age. The amount of the enzyme varied the probability of the child getting into trouble, but again, even the presence of the gene didn't guarantee the outcome. We can control our anger, to some extent, even during the most violent of times.

The genetic basis for our emotions can be mainly found in the realm of the brain, notably the limbic system and the amygdala, the seat of anger and fear. The amygdala is the part of the brain that helps determine the nature of anger and links negative and unpleasant sensations and experiences to a negative emotion, like anger. These links are stored in the amygdala. Though we might have some basic emotions with genetic components that we are born with, without life experiences and reference points, these basic emotions would not develop into the more complex psychological reactions and sensations we have. This is all part of a process we go through as human beings in our psychosocial development.

In a February 2011 issue of *Neuroscience News*, a story titled "Bullying, Genetics and Emotions: New Research Shows Links" documents the intricate dance of nature and nurture: "Genetics research into the emotional responses of bullying shows that many bullied victims that later experience more emotional problems have genetic similarities." Not all bullied children develop such later problems, according to the study for the August 2010 *Journal of the*

American Academy of Child and Adolescent Psychiatry, but there were indications in research done with 2,232 same-sex 5-year-old twins, with a later assessment at the age of 12, that showed genetic differences in the SS genotype of the 5-HTTLPR gene interacting with bullying and victimization to amplify later emotional problems. Additional studies showed that the SS genotype victims of relational aggression were also prone to experience depression.

So perhaps we are not the *tabula rasa*, or blank slate, that is favored by the "nurture" crowd—the theory that we are born without any built-in knowledge or mental content, and we are like a clean piece of paper upon which the story of our lives is written down. Perhaps we come with a few chapters already intact.

Evolution vs. Intelligent Design

The ultimate argument must begin with evolution and intelligent design. This author does not wish to use the term *Creationism* because it has religious connotations that simply don't help the argument in any kind of scientific sense. However, the concept of a type of intelligence, albeit not a human one, as First Cause does have links to scientific concepts discussed earlier.

Suffice it to say, though, the argument is really about who or what made us, when, and why. Evolution speaks of destiny, a fixed trajectory of human development throughout the course of millions and millions of years, yet one that is also influenced by adaptation, selection, and mutation. The idea that life evolved from a single cell organism speaks of both destiny and free will to adapt to the environment. The same, though, can be said for Intelligent Design. If there is indeed a First Cause/Creator/Intelligence behind everything that exists, there must then be some kind of purpose or destiny. Yet all around us we see things changing, expanding, and evolving. Is there a home for choice and free will in Intelligent Design?

Evolution is generational change of the inherited traits of an organism. As that organism evolves, it will develop traits that result from gene-environment interactions and lead to adaptations in bio-chemical, anatomical, and even behavioral makeup. Actual species can have an evolution of their own, called speciation, which involves an ancestral split that divides the original species line into new species, or new branches on an ever-expanding tree of life. But it all starts with one common ancestor from which all species are evolved.

Heritable traits such as eye color and body shape are under genetic control. Phenotypes are sets of observable traits that make up the structure of a particular organism, including the inherited behavioral aspects. These are the traits that DNA passes down from one generation to the next in a process of evolution that is often altered with potential mutations in the genetic makeup, leading to a different outcome, or adaptation throughout time to environmental stressors, which lead to specific traits that are amplified or suppressed. It's a lot more complex, but for the sake of this argument, evolution can suggest the actions of predeterminism, where a species or organism is dealt a specific set of physical cards with which to play the game of life. When it comes to free will, we might suggest that a species can choose its environment, and thus control some aspects of how it will adapt and evolve through time. Even interactions between different species can cause a sort of co-evolution, whereby both species develop matched adaptations. This is present in the cases of pathogens that require host bodies, but also in some predator-prey relationships where conflict is involved.

Other species may choose instead to develop along more co-operative lines, working together the way fungi grows on a plant's roots or within the plant cell itself, and exchanges important nutrients with its host.

We've all been privy to the ongoing religious versus scientific arguments about evolution, with the religious side believing that every human came from Adam and Eve thousands of years ago, and the science crowd clamoring for the Big Bang and the random emergence of life—and all points in between. But for this author, intelligent design takes on a more scientific potentiality, with a possible non-human consciousness or intelligence behind the intricate and complex structures, ratios, and patterns that make up everything that exists, from the massive galaxy to the tiny seed. As we discussed previously (see Chapter 4), there is too much complexity to ignore, and yet even evolution can fit nicely into a theory of intelligent design, for once again we are faced with the question of First Cause: If there was a Big Bang, who or what Banged it?

Evolutionary Destiny?

The amazing diversity of life produced throughout time by evolution speaks of a purpose or, at the very least, a blueprint by which the tree of life can expand. We know that we can breed certain species together, and other breeds we cannot, as if something knew and understood where the limits and boundaries of mutation and alteration began and ended. But all of life on earth, from the human to the plant to the animal, shares a common ancestor, as biological evolution tells us, and from that First Cause arose all of what we see today. Though the process of descent with modification, that common ancestor of all life exploded into the amazing diversity of trees and flowers, dogs and horses, people and insects, and in some far-off distant way we are all related: First Cause.

For those who ascribe to total random emergence of life, there are still the amazing diversity and complexity to contend with. Even if it was all just a crapshoot, whatever shot the craps did a bang-up job.

In *The Goldilocks Enigma*, author Paul Davies writes "Biological organisms are immensely complex.... To a physicist they look nothing short of miraculous. The many and diverse components function together in a coherent and amazingly orchestrated manner." The command base is encoded in the DNA, which gives the organism its marching orders via instructions through intermediary molecules that use an optimal mathematical code to convert, as Davies puts it, "software instructions into hardware products with customized functionality." This appearance of design is one of the "defining hallmarks of life." To Davies, it is hard to not then ask the question: Is there a Designer, and who or what is it?

But Davies is careful to distinguish between the evolution of life and the emergence of life when discussing the Intelligent Design theory. Emergence is how life got here in the first place. Evolution is how it developed into what it looks like today. Just because the emergence of life cannot yet be explained, we cannot automatically label it miraculous. "We can discuss the evolution of life only on the basis that life already exists," Davies states, wondering if life's beginning is an "irreducible" gap that might be home to the actions of an intelligent designer, which he does not agree with, or just a truth we have yet to discover with our modern scientific means. Even the Big Bang doesn't have to require a miracle or a plan, and could have occurred within the scope of known physical laws, and those intelligent design of those laws accepts that the universe runs itself according to such laws. Everything, then, that happens in the universe has a natural explanation.

But that still doesn't bring us to the one truth that evades us still: First Cause. And once again we are faced with the daunting task of not knowing what that Cause was, or what its intentions, if any, might have been. We are instead forced to work with the materials we have at hand, in the form of our own bodies, life around us, and the grander cosmos, seeking out as many indicators of a method to the proverbial madness.

We evolve, from childhood to adulthood. From immature to mature (hopefully). From little to big. As the old axiom states, "as above, so below." If we evolve why not the entirety of life itself?

Life is thought to have begun some 3.8 billion years ago, with human lineages diversifying approximately 5 million years ago. We know this through:

··· **Radiometric dating,** *which uses half-life decay of radioactive elements that allow the dating of rocks and materials.*

··· **Molecular clocks**, which use the amount of genetic divergence between organisms to extrapolate backward to estimate dates.

··· **Stratigraphy**, which provides scientists with a sequence of events from which they extrapolate relative dates.

Along with the study of the geologic record, scientists are pretty sure the planet and life have been around a long, long time, and that humans didn't just spring out of a bush somewhere. Things evolved, slowly and painstakingly, changing, mutating, and adapting according to the climate, hostility of the environment, and presence of food and water sources. Even warring and survival of the fittest served the natural selection of the strongest stock for many species, increasing their genetic hopes of continued survival. Natural selection is said to be a simple and mechanical process, the result of heredity, variation, and differential reproduction, all of which allow for adaptations that are beneficial to future generations, but certainly don't lead to perfection. Genetic variation in a population due to mutation may be random, but natural selection does seem to act upon that variation in a way that appears nonrandom, because variants that aid in survival and reproduction are more likely to become common than less likely. Thus, it is not a random process, and its only goal is to assist the species involved to better handle its habitat.

Ultimately the argument will always come back around to the compatibility of evolution and free will, moreso than evolution and intelligent design. Is choice—any choice—the result of free will or determinism? We human beings make choices every day, but we cannot know for sure if those choices come from a genetic predisposition or from the sheer will of our individual, unfettered minds. Charles Darwin, the grandfather of evolution, believed that free will was nonexistent, and thus not compatible with the theory of evolution. He also believed that adaptation wiped out the problem of intelligent design. But to this day, there is still a divide that cannot be closed between the belief that there was some purpose behind evolution, and that it was nothing but mechanistic, random, and chaotic activity. Though Darwin was convinced that free will was a delusion, and that motivation of action was mostly instinctive, other scientists allow for some free will based upon actual thought and conscious awareness processes, rather than instinctive, survival-based reaction.

Evolutionary biology is now being applied more and more to psychology and the study of human behavior, leaving less room for a belief that free will adds to the science itself. But ask any human being you know if he or she is operating out of pure, fixed, fated predeterminism or making his or her own purely free choices in life regardless of any environmental influence, overriding all genetic predispositions and tendencies, and he or she is bound to tell you more times than not that it is both. Humans are driven and compelled to make the choices they make, and when they aren't, they make those choices without thinking, and thus, from instinct.

Does life have a plan? Does existence have a destiny toward which it evolves ever forward? Do we humans have a blueprint by which our species will adapt and mutate and evolve into over generations of time?

In *The Purpose Guided Universe*, Bernard Haisch writes that "Without free will, humans, and other living things, would effectively be preprogrammed robots, their destiny immutably set—our destiny immutably sent—by the precise configuration of every atom and molecule in our bodies, which traces back to the previous history of each such particle, in principle all the way back to the beginning of the Universe." To Haisch, evolution of life forms was not only scientifically well-established, "but it is in fact the most logical way for a Creator to achieve his goal of creating experience through life-forms." A Creator that was capable of designing a few basic laws of physics that permitted the "tremendous complexity of life to evolve is, to me, more impressive than a Creator who has to tinker around with making creatures—with some striking failures along the way."

Haisch sees reductionism, causation working from the bottom up, as suggesting that the process of evolution had to have been traceable back to the atomic level. A purely mechanistic explanation for the emergence and evolution of organisms and bodies is fine with him, but only by accepting the intricacies we see all around us as being somehow "conducive" to the origin and evolution of life. That idea of conduciveness is where destiny and choice meet evolution and intelligent design in a game of four-square.

Biology is destiny, genetics is destiny, and even those who fully ascribe to evolution believe that it, too, is destiny, driving life toward some possible end goal of perfection, or maybe just a better way of survival within the environment. But biology includes the mind, thought, will, consciousness, and intention, all of which may allow for a whole lot of freedom to drive a part of that destiny in one direction or another, shifting and changing species into newer, stronger, better, faster models than their ancestors. Genetics cannot account for everything that happens to us, physically or behaviorally. Evolution can take detours.

So can we.

Six

Final or Forever: Beyond the Veil of Death

"We are not permitted to choose the frame of our destiny. But what we put into it is ours."
—Dag Hammarskjold

"How do geese know when to fly to the sun? Who tells them the seasons? How do we, humans, know when it is time to move on? As with the migrant birds, so surely with us, there is a voice within if only we would listen to it, that tells us certainly when to go forth into the unknown...."
—Elizabeth Kubler-Ross

"For he who lives more lives than one, more deaths than one must die."
—Oscar Wilde

Death is the great equalizer. Nobody gets out of here alive, as Doors singer Jim Morrison once quipped. We seem to have absolutely no choice as to when we will be born, or when we will die—not counting acts of suicide, of course. For those who believe death is the final act, destiny as well ends with that act. Each life has a beginning, a middle, and an end.

To those who suggest life goes on after death, as it had before we were born, the idea of destiny takes on a much larger role, reaching back into past lives and forward into lives to come, all of which are planned well in advance, with the purpose of teaching us great lessons and moving our soul along on a progression of growth, expansion, and perhaps, one day, full and eternal bliss with the source. At that point, we will no longer need to come back down to earth, so to speak, to try again, learn more, do more, be more.

We will be done.

The concept of reincarnation has been around for millennia, and each religion has its own take on the soul's progression.

Reincarnation Is Born

What we understand today as the classic description of reincarnation came from the doctrines of Eastern traditions as far back as the ninth century BC. The Upanishads were definitive about reincarnation, detailing the concept in writings between the seventh and fifth centuries BC, with other traditions such as Jainism and Buddhism adopting many of the tenets shortly afterward. As Buddhism spread throughout Asia, even the Chinese embraced the concept into Taoism after the third century BC.

Eventually, ancient cultures in the Mediterranean region would adopt their own ideas about reincarnation. Greek Platonists would write of the pre-existence of the soul in the celestial, which would then find a body to fall into because of an act of sin. In order to be liberated from that human body prison, the soul would have to purify itself through reincarnation. This process of purification is mirrored in the idea of many cultures that the progress made by the soul moves us toward reunification with bliss, the Divine, the One…God. Like the process of birth, death, and resurrection of the Western world, so much of what happened to a soul, its destiny, depended upon the actions taken in each life, which affected the next life in turn. Or, in the case of the Western religions, determined whether you ended up in heaven, hell, or somewhere in between. Always, there was great reward after death for those who behaved well during life.

Cause and effect.

Souls, to the ancient Egyptians, could travel into a new world and not return to earth if they chose. Some tribal cultures came to believe that a soul could be regressed into an animal form, if the person led a rotten life on earth. (Talk about a bad rap: Try having to come back as an aardvark!)

But it was the Eastern traditions that really set the foundation of what we today think of as karma and reincarnation, and having to go back, Jack, and do it again (wheels turnin' round and round, we go…).

Hinduism

The continuing cycle of birth, death, and rebirth is known as *samsara* in the ancient Hindu tradition. The soul, *atman*, leaves the body after death and may choose to be reborn into that of a plant, animal, or human. The Bhagavad Gita, the ancient sacred text of the Hindus that is a part of the *Mahabharata*, one of two Sanskrit epics depicting Hindu history, states that death is certain for the born, and birth is certain for the dead: "When one is born, death follows. When one dies, rebirth follows." This is true for every living being with a soul, atman, and the choice of how one behaves and acts during a lifetime determines the atman's future body. This is karma.

Karma is the Sanskrit word for action, and operates as the chain of continuous cause and effect, with moral implications based upon whether the cause was good or bad. This is simplified, but karmic action, if good, would lead to a good effect, and the same applies to bad behavior and action. Karma could be thought of as a moral law that, if one follows, leads to atman, or soul, getting one step closer to the desired end result, which is *moksha*, or liberation. The destiny was to get off the wheel of birth, death, and rebirth, and only through *dharma*, or proper path or right path, would this be achieved.

In the Gita, Lord Krishna has a deep and philosophical conversation with Pandava Prince Arjuna on a battlefield, before the Kurukshetra War. Arjuna is confused and seeks moral insight, which Lord Krishna imparts in the form of Yogic and Vedantic analogies and insights, which make up the text itself. Eventually Lord Krishna is disclosed as being the Supreme Being, *Svayam Bhagavan*, and allows Arjuna a glimpse of his divinity and universality.

This Vedantic scripture sets the stage for a belief in the foundational knowledge of yoga, which was imparted to humankind at creation. There is great focus on living a life on earth that is in alignment with greater truths and laws, and that through service and dharma, one can eventually shed the body, for the soul was permanent. A soul that followed dharmic order, which was considered universal, would progress toward the realm of the Supreme Being, where there was no ego, no false self.

Krishna speaks of the natural cycle of a human mortal as the wisdom of truly understanding what death is. It is not final. "Worn out garments are shed by the body; Worn out bodies are shed by the dweller within the body. New bodies are donned by the dweller, like garments." (Bhagavad Gita, 2:22). Man's final destiny then would be the merging of the soul, or atman, with *Brahman*, the eternal, unchanging, infinite Supreme. After that, the cycle would no longer be needed. One could rest in the eternal and transcendent reality.

The Puranas, another sacred Hindu text, take the whole idea of reincarnation to a whole new level. These narratives tell the history of creation to the end of the universe itself and describe in detail the cosmology of the Hindu. When it comes to reincarnation, the Garuda Purana gets very detailed about what one will come back as in the next life, based upon what his or sin sin in this life was.

For example, one who kills a cow will meet with a destiny of a hump-backed imbecile. If you steal food, you come back as a rat. If you commit vice, you come back as a village pig. If you are passionate, you come back as a "lustful horse." The Garuda Parana states: "Thus the makers of bad karma, having experienced the tortures of hell, are reborn with the residues of their sins, in these stated forms." The residues of their sins are the karmic action upon earth, and those causes end up with some very drastic and rather extreme effects to those of us who are used to a lesser punishment for something like stealing food! Coming back as a rat may be extreme, yes, but it served as a powerful deterrent to committing the crime in the first place, thus giving humans more motivation to live good and moral lives. The soul could be reborn innumerable times, and in numerous bodies, depending on the state of consciousness of the individual.

Varying philosophies had their own concepts of how atman could eventually, through karmic destiny, achieve union with Brahman, but the basic belief was that one's actions and behaviors had consequences that lasted beyond just one life. However, we have to keep in mind that the person himself or herself is not what is reborn into a new life, but the soul, the atman, with the impressions and implications of the karmic past, but not the personality or physicality of the body that carried it in the last life.

The Upanishads

Another set of Hindu philosophical texts are the Upanishads, of which more than 200 are known to exist. They are often attributed to a number of authors, including women, but all have been translated from original oral traditions. The Upanishads are considered one of the world's great sacred text collections, and along with the Gita and the Brahmasutra make up the foundation of later Hindu schools of philosophy that include Vedanta. The texts of the Upanishads, which are associated with one of the five Vedas or Vedic texts (Rigveda, Krishna Yajurveda, Samaveda, Shukla Yajurveda, and Atharvaveda) were the first to clearly formulate the idea of karma in action and cause and effect. In the *Brihadaranyaka* Upanishad, we are told: "According as one acts, according as one behaves, so does he become. The doer of good becomes good. The doer of evil becomes evil. One becomes virtuous by virtuous action, bad by bad action." Samsara, and reincarnation, then, is really all about reaping what one sows until all karmic debt over lifetimes is paid off. And the self has no choice but to keep on entering a new earth body until it gets it right.

Ultimately, the goal or final destiny is unification with Brahman, universal spirit. This is described as the fabric and core and destiny of all existence, manifest and un-manifest. Atman aspires to be Brahman, and the earth is the proving ground for just how much closer soul gets to Source with each go-around.

Buddhism

The Buddhist doctrine of reincarnation is similar to other Eastern traditions, but in Buddhist texts there is no "soul" or consciousness that is permanent or that moves from one life to the next. Buddhism teaches, instead, that *anatta*, or *anatman*, is "no soul," or "no self." The self that we think of, to Buddha, is really ego, personality, and self-ness, which is created by our bodies, beliefs, and ideas to give us a sense of identity or distinctive personality. Beyond this, there is nothing. The self is just an idea, a mental construct, and, in truth, what we are is constantly changing and impermanent.

That does not mean there is no concept of rebirth in Buddhism. There is, and karma, as action, is involved, but to the Buddhist, the "same person" is not somehow integrated into a new form. Instead, the physical body dies, but the energies within it take another form, another shape, but Buddha taught that our bodies do this on a continuous basis even while we are alive. In every moment, there is birth, decay, and death of the body in some regard. Nothing really gets to survive or be carried over into the next moment. It is all new, but the self, the ego, sees "renewal" in this process.

Rebirth to Buddhists is more of a belief in causality, and the causation of the present life can be carried into the next. To put it another way, how things end in one life can cause the beginning of the next life to be a certain way. There is connection, but not in the direct sense of Joe being reincarnated into Mary, and carrying with him all the karma he built up in his previous 20 lives. In the sacred Buddhist text collection, the *Pali Tipitaka*, the example of chitta works well to describe this. *Chitta* are the feelings, consciousness, and mental formations that make up "mental acts." A chitta will arise, exist, and then break up, giving way to another chitta, which also then falls away, and the flow is continuous. But each chitta will transfer its perceptions, emotions, and formations to those that follow, creating a *chittasantana*, or a continuum of mind. This creates an identity that carries on even as the physical body and actual personality do not.

Karma is not fate, but changeable actions, thoughts, and words. Human character is based upon the thoughts, actions, and words, either good or bad, accumulated over a lifetime.

Traditional Buddhism does teach of different realms of existence, 10 in all, with Buddha at the top as the enlightened Bodhisattva, who remains upon earth to teach wisdom, all the way down to the hellish, depraved men of earth. These are not actual physical worlds so much as mental ones, and karma has a lot to do with where a person is along the path from hell to enlightenment. Man creates his own hell, and his own heaven, and character and karma determine which.

So what does live beyond death to the Buddhist? Buddha taught about deeds having influence and being inherited beyond physical death, and that karma can indeed pass from one life into another, positing a causal nature between what is done in one life and what happens in the next. But the "self" does not pass on so much as there is constant transformation and impermanence. In the Garland Sutra (10), the Mahayana Buddhist sutra that explores the teachings and deeds of the Buddha Gautama, Buddha teaches that:

> "According to what deeds are done
> Do their resulting consequences come to be;
> Yet the doer has no existence..."

Instant Karma's Gonna Get You

What is karma?

In Indian religious traditions, karma represents actions and deeds. These actions and deeds spin the wheel of cause and effect, in a cycle that is called *samsara*, and only when karmic debt is released or paid in full can true moksha, or liberation from the wheel, be achieved.

Most Westerners seem to think of karma in a mockish sense, often using the concept to hope for the punishment of others' sins (as in, "her karma will catch up with her"). There is truth to this simplification. Karma does effect the past, the present, and the future, and the fruits of one's actions are called karma-phala. Karma is not punishment, then, but simply the resultant consequences of one's actions. Karma is reaping what you sow, and that can be good, or it can be evil.

The Buddha taught that inequalities in humankind, such as disease, disaster, poverty, and suffering, were partly heredity, environment, and karma. Our past actions and deeds did lead us to current happiness or misery. When the Buddha was asked about why some humans must suffer and others not, he answered, "All living beings have Karma as their own, their inheritance, their congenital cause, their kinsman, their refuge. It is Karma that differentiates beings into low and high states." Our "karmic tendencies" are inherited throughout the course of lifetimes and have great influence on the current existence, thus the need to release oneself from "karmic debt" by doing good deeds in the current lifetime.

However, Buddha did not ascribe to determinism entirely, stating that although karma does account for a lot of what we experience, it does not account for it all. Buddha was no fatalist. Karma was only one of 24 laws operating in the Buddhist philosophy, but indeed one to be taken seriously. And one's surroundings, circumstances, and influences also helped to shape karma, giving a sense of free will to the cause and effect chain. One could use karma as a deterrent against doing evil, or a motivator to do good. One had choice, even with past Karmic influence weighing in.

Another Buddhist teaching has karma as action, and Vipaka as fruit or reaction. In the sacred Buddhist scripture "Samyutta Nikaya" (the third of five nikayas, or collections, in the "Sutta Pitaka" of Theravada Buddhism), we are told:

"According to the seed that is sown,
so is the fruit you reap there from.
Doer of good will gather good.
Doer of evil, evil reaps,
Down is the seed and thou shalt taste
The fruit thereof."

Sounds awfully similar to the Christian teachings of "do unto others," and "you reap what you sow." Also note the interesting similarities with the law of attraction teachings of cause and effect, and the power of words, thoughts, and intentions to actually create a person's reality. Same message, different lingo.

This implies that there is an aspect of the mental "self" that carries over, even if the physical person has no recollection in the new life of anything that mental self did in the last life. Unlike some

Hindu beliefs where someone comes back in the next life specifi-cally as a particular creature, or class of human, depending on the person's sins and deeds, Buddhism focuses more on an entirely non-physical aspect that carries over. In the Tibetan Book of the Dead, it gets a bit more explicit, describing what happens after death. There is a "mental body of instincts" that cannot die, which one might experience in the *bardo*, or intermediary state between one incarnation and the next. Buddhism is frustratingly unclear as to just what this mental body might really be. It is not self, or ego, or even soul or consciousness, yet the Book of the Dead tells us that we should not fear the visions after death, for that aspect of us that continues on cannot be harmed in death.

The Chinese tradition of Taoism has much of the same confu-sion as to what passes on beyond death. The Tao-te Ching, the sacred scripture of Chuang Tzu, mentions that birth is not a begin-ning, death is not an end, and that there is existence without limi-tation (space), and continuity without a starting point (time). The scripture suggests that there is a timeless, spaceless "void" that one passes out of at birth and back into at death, similar to the more sci-entific Zero Point Field, or the metaphysical Akasha. From the field we emerge, and to the field we will return. Source is unchanging.

The Western Traditions

When it comes to the big three Western religious traditions, it was only around the 19th century that reincarnation even became an "acceptable" subject to discuss. Before then, the Abrahamic re-ligions tried to avoid, or drastically alter, the teachings of the East to fit into emerging concepts of what would become a very different view of God, man, and the cycle of life and death.

Certainly, the "reaping what you sow" aspect of karmic law made it into the Western traditions, if only in the form of sin and punishment by an angry, judgmental God.

Judaism believes in an afterlife, and that death is not the end of a human existence. The teachings of the Torah, however, serve to emphasize this life, now, and how there are immediate rewards and punishments for sins and behaviors in the present, with a much more abstract view taken of future punishment beyond death. Orthodox Jews may acceptably believe that good souls end up in a heavenly state, and that the souls of the wicked can either cease to exist at death, or be tormented in a sort of hell on earth.

In the Torah, there are numerous references to the dead being reunited with loved ones after death. The wicked are not permitted this grace. There is also a fundamental belief in resurrection of the dead, which will occur upon the return of the Messiah and the World to Come, called the Olam Ha-ba, but there seems to be some maneuvering room for a true belief in reincarnation. The Olam Ha-ba can also be looked upon as a higher state or realm of existence, and in the Talmud, Israel is given its share in this higher realm or World to Come. With a caveat, that is: Righteous people will be given a greater share in the World to Come than your average Joe. Sinners lose their place in the higher realm, much like the Eastern concept of karma, but ultimately, the focus remains on what good can be done in the present life.

Mystical Judaic schools of thought believe that reincarnation is not a one-shot deal, but an ongoing progression or process in which the souls of the righteous are reborn to engage in the mending of the world, or *tikkun olam*. For traditional Hebrew teachings, though, only allusions are made in the Torah to *gilgal ha'ne'shamot*, which means literally the transmigration of souls,or reincarnation, the purpose of which would be to achieve a goal that could not be reached in the life before it, or accept reward for a life well lived and one that served the Creator. One quote often referred to is from Daniel 12:13: "...Now go your way to the end and rest, and you shall arise to your destiny at the end of days." This suggests resurrection and a final destiny, though, more than a cycle of birth, death, and rebirth.

Islam understands resurrection, or the transmigration of souls, in a similar way, with the idea that Allah might reward with justice those who did good deeds, and give painful torment to those who disbelieved and committed sins. But this is not to be thought of as a cycle of returning to earth in a new body. Islam firmly believes in the return to Him, Allah, alone and that there will be a Day of Resurrection for those who are deemed fit. Allah can bring someone back to life and cause someone to die, and all will be returned again to Allah in the end.

Allah will confront each individual at death, and that person's deeds and actions will be weighed in a scale called *mizan*, the results determining whether they will delivered to *firdaws* (Paradise) or *jahannam* (Hell). Thus, the actions and beliefs of Muslims during the present life alone indicate their fate after physical death. Many modern Muslims, though, have somewhat accepted reincarnation as part of their individual beliefs, mainly because of the difficulty of accepting that humans only have one shot to get it right, and then reap the heavenly rewards or the hellish ones. The idea of having many chances to get it right holds great appeal, as it allows for improvement, learning, and wisdom to be put into action.

Jews and Muslims alike look to a final reward for appropriate and righteous behavior after death, which will come as eventual resurrection and immortality, and both traditions emphasize good works and deeds in the present life for more than just the sake of afterlife rewards. Moral life alone was a good enough motive for good behavior and had its own rewards in service to others and to the Creator.

Certainly Christianity follows this same trajectory, with the promise of heaven, hell, or purgatory based upon the final judgment of sins after death. However, the New Testament is filled with references to possible reincarnation:

- ··· "Rabbi, who sinned, this man or his parents, that he be born blind?" (John 9:2)

- ··· "No one can see the Kingdom of God unless he is born again...." (John 3:3)

··· *"And if you are willing to accept it, he (John the Baptist) is
the Elijah who has come." (Matthew 11:14)*

These are but a few of the many quotes that suggest a definite belief in life after physical death, although the emphasis on most New Testament teachings was of spiritual rebirth rather than physical. Statements such as "Do unto others," "As you judge, so you will be judged," and "He who lives by the sword, shall die by the sword" also speak of karmic law, and most religious scholars agree that the older teachings of the East are found throughout Western traditions, albeit in veiled references. Galatians 6:7 says: "Do not be deceived; God cannot be mocked. A man reaps what he sows," and this concept of cause and effect, or paying the consequences for ones actions, is found throughout the New Testament.

Some scholars hypothesize that reincarnation was written out of the Bible, most likely removed during the Fifth Ecumenical Council in AD 553 Constantinople, but there is no proof of this. Reincarnation would simply not jive with the accepted belief that people who followed Christ must try to live without sin, to avoid the consequences at Final Judgment. There is no mention of getting a few chances to clear the Karmic slate. In Christianity, you try your damndest to get it right the first time.

Is there destiny and free will for Jews, Muslims, and Christians? Of course, the final destiny occurred after death, either as resurrection or union with the Creator for all eternity. Free will was what guaranteed you got there—or didn't.

Modern Thought

Karma and reincarnation certainly play a much bigger role in the metaphysics and New Age beliefs of today. From a variety of religious traditions, we pick and choose our beliefs until we find the perfect fit, and more times than not that fit will include the concepts of cause and effect, and having the opportunity to learn over many lifetimes. But modern pop culture is rampant with belief in ghosts and life after death, and for many there is not only a dis-tinction, but a contradiction, between the existence of ghosts and reincarnation.

Life after death, which has been studied in countless books, and portrayed in countless more movies and television shows, brings up visions of going into the light to join loved ones in eternal bliss, if that is indeed your fate. Many people who claim to believe in life after death may also think they believe in reincarnation, but there is a line that distinguishes the two. For many religiously in-clined believers, life after death ends in heaven or in hell. For the more metaphysically minded, it may mean leaving the body and becoming pure consciousness and returning from "some"-thing to "every"-thing. This speaks of finality, and that there is only one life, and one death, and after that death you go back to Source.

For some, it ends there. But those who ascribe to reincarnation take it one step further: that the soul or essence or consciousness can then choose to enter a new body and have a new "human" experience on earth. This choice can be made during the time one spends in that "bardo," or in-between state, and the reconciliation with loved ones can be temporary if the soul then chooses to go back down to the proving grounds and learn new lessons. Thus, the ultimate destiny of a soul can take many lifetimes to be unveiled, as opposed to one lifetime, and final bliss beside the Lord or Godhead of many religious traditions (or eternal damnation in the "other" place, which we hope to avoid at all costs!).

Thousands of people have reported near-death experiences (NDEs) and for many the experience included instruction to go back to earth and fulfill a destiny. The implication is that we go to a holding area where we are with those we loved, who surprisingly look the same as they did during their lifetimes, and we can then either stay, or go back if we are not yet done with our life purpose. Often, angels and guides, or a higher power within the white light reported, help us make that determination. If the determination is we go back, we are miraculously revived on the operating room table with a newfound lust for life and a new sense of meaning and direction.

Near-death experiences tend to have commonalities among those who experience them, which include the sense of a higher presence, a tunnel leading to a white light, the presence of loved ones greeting them, and the review of life events and experiences. Scientific proof of these experiences, and even life after death itself, is in short supply, but in a book called *Evidence of the After-life*, radiation oncologist Dr. Jeffrey Long writes about his years of research involving some 1,600 near-death cases he studied while fighting for the lives of cancer victims. His research made him a believer after he found no other way to explain the consistencies of what experiencers reported. His book catalogs the stories and is a must-read for those who want the most current "scientific" look at NDEs. Other studies have examined the possibility of conscious-ness existing after physical brain death, but conclusions are elusive.

Still, to those who have experienced an NDE, no proof is need-ed. And to many, destiny and choice play a role in what happens not only in life, but in death.

There may, in fact, be two deaths to consider: the physical death, or death of the body, which returns to dust and earth, and the "spiritual" death that is symbolic of the separation from God that occurs when humankind sins or falls prey to arrogance, greed, and war. Even an individual can suffer a spiritual death, while still physically alive, and lose his or her soul to the devil, so to speak. Even if the body perishes, the spirit continues, striving toward per-fection, Nirvana, totality, all-or-nothingness, depending upon your beliefs. And perhaps it is that spirit that hangs out for too long in the bardo, wondering what to do next, seen as a "ghost" to those who are still alive, yet not yet incarnated into a new being.

Those who believe in ghosts sometimes struggle to find room for reincarnation in their belief system. Yet the two can coincide. Ghosts are often thought to be the spirit of dead Aunt Bessie, but new theories stretch far beyond that simplistic explanation. And even if a ghost is dear dead Aunt Bessie, she may just be stuck in the between, not eager to leave the life she left behind or venture forth into the new life. Ghosts do not have to be the "eternality" of a person's soul or spirit wandering aimlessly at the location of the person's traumatic death. If we only accept the traditional explanation of a ghost as a dead person's spirit that continues to walk between worlds in the same clothing, looking the same as the person did in life, with even the same characteristics, that would suggest that once we die we still maintain some semblance of physicality in appearance. And yet, our bodies die and decay. Science proves this. Open a coffin and prove it to yourself. What remains may either be an energy that exists in another realm or dimension, or a construct of our own minds, where we still "see" the dead as they were in life.

Again, if we reincarnate, we do not come back looking like we did before. And if upon death, only our soul remains, it would not have a physical appearance as it was "clothed" in during life. So how can ghosts and reincarnation co-exist? The answer quite simply requires a different understanding of what a ghost may be. I looked around some paranormal forums to see what those who believed in both had to say, and it was pretty generic:

··· "Reincarnation is the second life of a spirit, and a ghost is a spirit that does not yet want to leave the old life behind...."

··· "We come into this world to learn lessons, and then once we do, we die and move on to another incarnation and more lessons. A ghost could be in a place of waiting, and we see it as it was in the former life, until it chooses to be reincarnated again...."

··· "If ghosts are the lost or departed souls of the living, then perhaps they stick around for a while.... After the soul finishes what it needs to do in it's current life, it moves on...."

··· And my favorite: "It's a big universe. Lots of options."

Ghosts and Reincarnation

I decided to ask one of the most respected paranormal researchers around, who also happens to be my writing and business partner in ParaExplorers, Larry Flaxman, about this possible conflict between the existence of ghosts and reincarnation. Larry is the founder and senior researcher of ARPAST, the Arkansas Paranormal and Anomalous Studies Team, the most well-equipped and scientifically focused "paranormal" research group out there.

MARIE: Most people today believe in both ghosts and reincarnation. Yet often people report ghosts as appearing in the afterlife just as they did in this life. As a scientific/paranormal researcher who often investigates "haunted" locations, do you believe in ghosts? If so, what do you believe they are?

LARRY: Excellent questions, and one in which my response could likely fill a novel. My own personal belief regarding what is popularly termed "ghosts" or "spirits" is that "they" are a phenomenon that has defied rational explanation—and very likely may continue to do so for the foreseeable future. Even after conducting hundreds of scientific paranormal investigations, I still have too many unresolved questions in my mind to form any type of educated hypothesis regarding "their" constitution or make-up.

Certainly there are theories and beliefs—however, none that I can fully support as being absolutely, unequivocally, correct. Are what we believe to be the spirits of the departed simply one's own consciousness somehow being projected or recorded? Are we witnessing some type of energy transfer? Can the countless number of experiences throughout the ages all be explained away as psychological trickery, i.e., pareidolia or cognitive overload?

I truly believe that until we have a better understanding of the mechanisms and dynamics surrounding the experiential and anecdotal evidence regarding "ghosts," it would be pointless to attempt to explain what "they" might be. Furthermore, until legitimate, mainstream science takes a profound interest in the study of paranormal phenomena, the answers as to what "they" are will continue to elude us.

MARIE: Do you believe in reincarnation?

LARRY: Absolutely. I've been fascinated with the concept of reincarnation ever since reading the book *Children Who Remember* by Dr. Ian Stevenson. Dr. Stevenson's work with young children and their amazing abilities to recall memories, historical specifics, and languages far advanced for their ages has convinced me of the possibility of reincarnation.

While some may consider reincarnation to be unconventional, the idea is actually not all that unusual. Several major religions, among them Judaism, accept reincarnation as a viable modality. In fact, reincarnation is a central tenet of Kabbalah, and it teaches that we will return to this world in many incarnations until we have completed the specific tasks or "purpose" we were destined to do.

Transcending religious, metaphysical, or spiritual beliefs, among other things, the scientific laws of thermodynamics put into motion the concepts of energy transfer and entropy. Applying that model, upon physical death of the human "shell," our energy doesn't simply vanish or disappear; it transfers to another medium. Many believe that this notion certainly seems to support the idea of reincarnation.

MARIE: How can people reconcile the two beliefs?

LARRY: Personally, I believe that the concept of "ghosts" and "reincarnation" are wholly unrelated, hence one's ability to reconcile their belief against both is effectively nullified. If the concept of reincarnation holds to be true—and based upon a substantial amount of legitimate research it appears that it may be a viable possibility—then it would make sense that "ghosts" would never even enter the equation.

In other words, if life is truly a cycle, and corporeal death is in actuality a form of rebirth (or reincarnation into the next life), then how would the concept of "ghosts" even fit into the cycle? To me, this dichotomy greatly simplifies the reconciliation and allows for the separation and compartmentalization of one's spiritual beliefs and the belief in "ghosts" or "spirits."

Thermodynamics tells us that the energy we are made of does not cease to exist, even if our "solid" physical bodies do. That energy goes somewhere, either transforming into another state of energy or transferring into another thermodynamic system. Perhaps it is that surviving energy that is given the role of carrying on the quest of individual destiny, should it choose to do so. Where that energy goes and what form it takes still eludes us in a scientific, objective sense, but most people would agree they think they know that a part of them lives on, and has lived before. It's purely intuitive, subjective, and experiential—but it can feel just as real as anything the five senses can perceive.

Destiny, then, seems to happen on two levels. We live one life at a time, and that life has its own path, trajectory, and destiny, which we often discern through our goals, desires, and intuitions. Then we have the overall destiny of our soul's ongoing progression to perfection, bliss, all-or-nothingness, which can take 10 lifetimes or 10 thousand lifetimes—and all along the way, on both levels, grand and small, we have karma, action, and choice about how to get to each one—if we indeed ever do.

We also may have a choice in determining who we travel our soul journeys with—and why.

Seven

Soul Codes and Contracts: Are You My Soul Mate?

"Adapt yourself to the things among which your lot has been cast and love sincerely the fellow creatures with whom destiny has ordained that you shall live."
—Marcus Aurelius

"Nothing happens by chance, my friend...no such thing as luck. A meaning behind every little thing, and such a meaning behind this. Part for you, part for me, may not see it all real clear right now, but we will, before long."
—Richard Bach

If we have lived before, and will live again, does that mean our soul has a destiny encoded within it that, throughout the course of many existences, will unfold to full manifestation and culmination? The idea of soul destinies, codes, and contracts implies that we do indeed have a blueprint that we should be living in accordance with, and that when we deviate from that blueprint, we deviate from our authenticity and our destiny. As always we can choose to do either. And more times than not, those blueprints involve us meeting and interacting with key individuals who will contribute to our growth, and ultimately, our destiny.

Soul Codes

In his book, *Your Soul's Plan: Discovering the Life You Planned Before You Were Born*, author Robert Schwartz examines the experiences of individuals who believe their lives have been preplanned as their soul's agreement on how to best use the current incarnation to progress toward a destined outcome. The book looks at people who have found in their challenges, obstacles, and sufferings that they were living out a code that their own soul chose before birth, a code that held within it their purpose and path.

What is so interesting in these personal stories is how often other people are such a big part of that purpose and path. Schwartz's book looks at how soul codes are involved in issues such as being born to certain parents, alcoholism and addiction, physical illnesses and disabilities, and even accidents, and how these challenges play into choices we make before birth as to what challenges we will face in this lifetime. What may look like a tragedy to us is often rooted in the soul's previous decision to actually experience a particular life, in order to achieve growth and progress.

Soul Codes
Some aspects of a person's life are predestined—for example, someone who plans before birth to be born with a physical handicap that cannot be treated in any way.

Much more often, though, the life plan consists of a vast web of time lines or possibilities/probabilities. One chooses, though perhaps not consciously, which time line to travel based on one's free will decisions. If lessons are learned, they need not be repeated. If they are not learned, one may draw to oneself additional opportunities to master the planned lessons.

Let us take the example of a soul who plans before birth to learn to stand up for herself. Perhaps this is something the soul had difficulty with in previous lifetimes. This soul might plan to marry—say, at the age of 30—another member of her soul group whose plan is to learn to respect the wishes of others. Perhaps this is something he had difficulty with in past lives. These two souls know that the marriage is likely to be turbulent, but their intention is that it will foster the desired growth in both of them.

Let's say the woman, when she is 25, takes a job in which her employer treats her with a profound lack of respect. Now, let's say that she marshals her internal resources and makes a stand: She tells her employer that he must treat her with respect and kindness or she will quit. In that moment there is a tremendous increase in the woman's vibration. If she can sustain that vibration until she is 30, one of two things is likely to happen. Either she and the man she planned to marry never meet (the law of attraction does not bring them together) or they have only one date (there is no attraction due to the difference in their vibrations). Thus, the need for the planned challenge (the marriage) was obviated by the woman's ability to learn the intended lesson earlier in life.

This example demonstrates the interaction between free will and pre-birth planning.

One can find peace and forgiveness through intuiting whether an experience was planned, but it is perhaps even more helpful to adopt a position of complete non-resistance to all challenges, whether one believes them to have been pre-planned or not. Acceptance IS transmutation. This is another way of saying that all suffering is caused by our resistance to what happens, not by the events themselves.

People who do not learn what they planned to learn in a particular lifetime often feel after they return to the nonphysical realm that they would like to come back to "get it right." That one does so is not a punishment, but rather an opportunity to continue one's evolution—a process with no end.

Rob Schwartz is the author of Your Soul's Plan: *Discovering the Real Meaning of the Life You Planned Before You Were Born.* Learn more at www.yoursoulsplan.com/.

The concept of soul codes and soul plans does indeed help to explain some of life's greater tragedies and misfortunes. Would someone ask to be born blind, were it not a part of a bigger picture—a piece of that person's life puzzle that only his or her soul understood? Would someone wish to lose a child were it not again a link in the chain of lifetimes for both the child and the parents who are devastated, all three of them making choices beforehand to have just such a tragic experience?

The alternative is to believe that everything is random and we are powerless, with no choice in the matter of what we are born with and the cards we are dealt. To believe there is no previous decision on behalf of the soul is to accept that some people are born blind, others get cancer and die young, and others still become rich and happy and live to be 100, and it is a total crapshoot. Many people simply have a difficult time accepting that kind of position of powerlessness. It is more empowering to think that the challenges we are handed at birth, and throughout our lifetime, are all a part of a larger scenario that we agreed to take part in, albeit on a soul level.

Robert Schwartz writes in *Your Soul's Plan* about using mediums to help people uncover their "pre-birth plans," which often help the individuals finally understand not just tragic events, such as the loss of a spouse, but how coincidences really are not coincidences at all, and that people come into, and go out of, our lives for a reason. We may not like it, but there is a reason, and that reason, as one woman named Valerie's session with a medium named Deb

DeBari reveals, might even involve a loved one dying in an accident that was "planned on the other side." Valerie had experienced two tragic deaths, and wanted to know from Ms. DeBari if the latest death of her fiancé, D.C., was truly an accident.

Through the course of the session, Valerie was contacted by D.C.'s spirit, and he told her that he had known his life would not be long, and that he had a contract to die at an early age. Part of this came from his not respecting life enough and needlessly putting himself at risk. "A lot was carried over from past lives," he said, detailing how his actions and choices in past incarnations had led to his accident in the present one. He also indicated that he did not have to incarnate again right away, and could instead focus for a while on the lessons his recklessness taught him, so that he could be "better equipped" to find his purpose in the next.

Schwartz writes that D.C. referred during the session to "the forgetfulness each of us experience when we enter the earth plane. As eternal beings, we are well aware of the purposes of our lives before we incarnate." Unfortunately, when we finally do incarnate back on Earth, we often forget, permanently or temporarily, the reasons why we came back, and thus we are given a host of life challenges to help us remember and keep us on the path to our purpose.

Soul Contracts

Many of these life challenges involve people we often feel as though we've known before, or people who truly push our buttons, make us crazy, or stretch us to grow in ways we've never imagined. We may have actually made soul contracts with these people before birth, both agreeing to experience certain things during the new incarnation that will serve both souls' paths toward spiritual progress.

Do we choose our parents, so we can specifically deal with issues each of them may present before us? Do we choose who our children will be, who our siblings will be, and who we will marry? Along the soul's path, obviously certain challenges will require that we are surrounded with those who are aligned with, or opposed to, the challenges. We call these people our soul mates, and will discuss that in a bit. But first, we all sit down at the table before our collective births and decide that we are going to interact after birth, in an intricate dance of mingled destines and entangled life blueprints.

The idea behind soul contracts is that there is a part of us that is always aware of not just past lives, but future destinies and which one we most hope to move toward. This is our soul, of course, and, though our conscious mind has little or no awareness of this hidden knowledge, our soul retains it before, during, and after birth, and we use intuition, inner guidance, and even some outer wisdom at times, to tune into this information and keep us on our path.

Think of yourself as a spiritual being having a human experience. The spiritual part of you knows where you need to go, and with whom you need to go there. And it knows this way ahead of time. Thus, you have benchmarks along the way that, if you are paying attention, will keep you moving forward, progressing through life lessons, and hopefully overcoming obstacles so that you don't have to go back and redo it again the next time around.

Astrologers often say that the time, place, and date of our births create a resonance or vibrational pattern that act as a path for our quest on Earth. We then use our intuition, instinct, and inspired choices to meet those we need to meet to help us get from point A to B, and we use the same gifts to help us make decisions that put us in the right places at the right times to be given the next piece of the puzzle of our lives.

Having a soul contract with someone does not mean he or she is going to make you happy. In fact, a soul contract can involve being in relationship with someone who truly causes you great suffering until the contract is played out on both ends. An example of this is a woman who just cannot get along with her mother. Her mother is domineering and controlling, and always has been, and the woman is suffering because of it. She is anxious, is depressed, allows others to treat her like a doormat, and is even beginning to suffer physical symptoms that she knows in her heart are related to her horrible relationship with her mother.

Then one day, the woman just has had enough, and explodes in a furious rage toward her mother. A huge fight escalates, but as the hours pass, the dialogue suddenly becomes different. The daughter finds herself listening—really listening—to her mother describe how horribly she was treated when she was a child by a mother who only cared about herself, and the daughter begins to feel empathy and compassion for the older woman. The mother, on the other hand, begins to feel a strong sense of shame and guilt for passing her anger onto her daughter, who deserved only love. Suddenly, a door is opened for true reconciliation and understanding. Two years later, after a lot of work and therapy, the daughter considers her mother her best friend.

The soul contract has been fulfilled, forgiveness and reunion have occurred, and growth has been achieved on both ends.

This does not mean that soul contracts always end with the people involved being buddies and loving each other again. In fact, a soul contract could end with two people realizing they've served out their purposes in each other's lives, and that it is time to leave. This is sometimes the case with marriages, where two spouses are constantly at each other's throats, pushing each other's buttons and making each other crazy. Until the lesson is learned on both ends, though, the contract stays valid. Once both parties realize what they are doing to themselves, and to each other, they can forgive and move on, thus ending their soul contract with each other and moving forward to new lessons and experiences. Holding on to someone with whom your soul contract has ended is a matter of choice. These two people may continue to be friends, or never be in contact again. As long as the predestined contract is played out, it is up to them what is best.

Another example of a collective soul contract might be an event in history where a gunman opens fire on a crowd of people in a restaurant, killing seven and wounding five others. We may look at this as a horrific tragedy that occurred at random, or because of the choices made by a mentally imbalanced man with a gun, but those who believe in soul contracts would instead say that each of the people involved, including the survivors and spectators, agreed to be exactly where they were at the time. Those who were killed were serving a much greater purpose than our small minds could wrap themselves around. It was all a part of a contract all of the individuals involved agreed to long before they were all incarnated, and one that, although appearing tragic, may have been the catalyst to propelling each of them toward their own individual destinies.

There is no proof that this is what happens. No objective, scientific proof. But it is a much more agreeable belief than random acts of violence, and it might help explain why, just why, we truly feel sometimes when we meet a new person that we've known his or her all our lives. Has this happened to you?

Soul Mates

You meet someone, perhaps at a party or event, and you feel as though you have known this person for a lifetime, maybe even 10 lifetimes. Soul mates are people we have supposedly had interactions with before, and who are now back in our lives to help us achieve certain goals and teach us different lessons. I have had many experiences meeting people who I truly believed I'd known before, and they proved instrumental in my growth. But our ideas of soul mates are often distorted by dating Websites and love gurus who try to get us to believe that a soul mate is a person we are destined to walk side by side through life with. This is not always the case.

Imagine if we truly have known thousands of people in previous incarnations. Many of those are people who were not nice to us, whom we did not love and adore, and who maybe even pissed us off more than they pleased us. Soul mates—real soul mates—can be in our lives to make us happy, and to make us miserable, and it all is a part of our destiny—and theirs.

The media and dating worlds have long driven into our brains that soul mates are the people we have love relationships with, and this may be the case, as often our closest relationships are soul mate relationships. Those we choose to be born to, our parents, and the families we incarnate into, as well as our friendships, love relationships, and even our enemies can all be soul mates to us, each with specific roles they will play in our spiritual development. That is not to say everyone is our soul mate, but that these special people can come in many shapes and forms, even total strangers who show up at the exact right time and place to propel us forward into our next great adventure.

I had just such an experience as a young girl in a local public library, when a sweet elderly Japanese man came up to me and asked me if I intended to read the armload of books I was holding. We struck up a nice conversation about books, learning, and education, and before he parted my company, he said to me, "You are going to be a great diplomat one day." I never forgot that statement, and oddly enough ended up joining many political and activist groups shortly afterward, where I found I had a gift for diplomacy and bringing people together. To this day, I remember that event and that man's words, and realize that he was recognizing me as someone he needed to help push along. I am still one hell of a diplomat, often finding the middle ground between two extremes.

I also recall in my mid-20s meeting a young woman named Patrice on a new job and thinking that I had known her forever. We became fast friends and embarked together on a journey of discovering past lives, meditation, and metaphysics, as this was the height of popularity of Shirley MacLaine's book *Out on a Limb*, which opened the doorway for many to the idea of soul mates and past lives. That friendship lasted a few years before she moved to Boston and we lost touch forever.

Soul mates can come into our lives for moments, for months, or for years. Some stay forever, as couples who truly believe they have found their life mate will tell you. Some stay just long enough to do what it was they planned before birth, and then they move on.

Some end up being our enemies, betrayers, and destroyers, who come into our lives to force us to deal with issues of the past that we continue to deny, suppress, or bury. Or they come to push our buttons until we finally get to the breaking point and dismantle the button entirely. Or they come to mirror our own fears, flaws, and issues back to us so that we can identify them, admit and own up to them, and process through them once and for all. Otherwise, those issues will come back in the next life, along with those soul mates, although not in the same form. Your brother could come back as your son, your spouse could come back as your sister, or you could be dealing with new souls entirely who are now connected to you for your own good, and for theirs.

Twin Flames

Soul mates are often confused for twin flames. Whereas a soul mate can be in your life for only the length of time your "contract" with him or her is active, a twin flame is more of a true "soul's mate," someone who has more impact on your life overall. Those who believe in twin flames tell us that when our soul enters the physical plane upon incarnating, it divides in half, into a male and female aspect, and that throughout our lifetime we long to reunite with our "other half." Perhaps our twin flame is even encoded in our DNA, and we may not find our twin flame in this life. In fact, it may take many lifetimes to reunite once twin flames are split asunder. Or we may get lucky and find our twin flame right away, vowing to spend the rest of our life in blissful satisfaction of knowing we found "the one."

Each twin flame still has a complete soul of its own, but that soul is imbalanced, favoring the female or male energy, and the goal is to find that wholeness of balance with the other half—our counterpart, the yin to our yang. This is not about men and women, but about divine energy that is both masculine and feminine in nature, and only whole when both those natures are balanced and in harmony.

This doesn't mean we are all walking around with half a soul. No, our souls are complete and whole, so twin flames or twin souls are really polar mirrors of our own soul, the opposite of our soul, or even the compliment to our soul. Think of actual physical twins, each with their own physical bodies and organs; they share a special bond that only they can feel, a bond that sets them apart from all others and can only be made complete with one another.

Allegedly, finding our twin flame is a rare and precious occurrence, and there is no guarantee that one will do so in this go-around at life. Our souls, if indeed they are evolving over many lifetimes, may be in a state of ongoing preparation to reunite with their twins, but still have a lot of learning and growing to do on their own first. The more open and evolved a soul is, the closer it will be to finding its twin and becoming one again.

Reunited and it Feels So Good...

Whereas soul mates can be our spouses, children, parents, friends, colleagues, or even complete strangers, twin flames are special because they are the other half of our divine being. Many people long to find their twin flame, and wonder if they can help the reunion along, or if it is all in divine timing and out of our hands. Suggestions abound for how to make this happen faster, or make it more likely to happen, with everything offered from meditation, looking for synchronicities with certain people, or just being open to whoever comes our way. But there is the belief as well that before one can reconnect to his or her twin flame, he or she must do the hard work of learning specific lessons and overcoming issues that keep them "separated" in the first place, and those must be achieved solo—alone. Each soul must find a way as well to become balanced and in harmony with its own divine energies before finally joining back up with the opposing half. All of this is simply spiritual work that a soul must do for evolutionary growth.

Perhaps we meet our twin flame in consciousness long before our twin flame comes into our lives in a physical sense. Only when we are at a level of conscious awareness when we are truly ready for such an intense reunion can we then pave the way for our twin flame to show up for real, in the flesh. This requires working on the ego, opening to resonant energies of those who vibrate at our same frequency, letting go of past hurts and old beliefs that do not serve us, and forgiving anyone that needs forgiving, including ourselves. If this is the hard work that must be done to open the door for the twin flame to enter our lives, we can honestly see why so few people have the experience of reunion. Who wants to do all that inner excavating and cleaning out of the subconscious, where the cobwebs of the past are thick as caramel and the perceptions and beliefs we hold fast to only serve to keep us from any kind of growth?

The One—NOT!

One of the problems with this kind of belief—that there is one and only one twin flame out there, or soul twin—is that it takes all the choice out of finding someone with whom we really want to spend our life. If it is all predestined, written in the stars, and decided before birth, then does that mean those people out there who have yet to find "the one" are doomed to maybe never find that person? Is there only one person we can truly be happy with, or is this all wishful thinking, not to mention a great selling point for dating gurus and Websites intended to help us find "the one"?

The Hebrew word for "the One" is *B'shert*, or beloved, and perhaps we can choose who will become our beloved instead of waiting for just one person to satisfy our heart's many needs. For what of those who find their "one," only to lose that person to death or divorce, and go on to find someone else to love, perhaps even moreso? That would mean there are many "ones" out there for us, depending on our needs, desires, and choices, and where we are at in our emotional and spiritual growth. "The one" for a teenager may not be "the one" for her when she is 35 and ready to settle down.

In an article for *Match.com* titled "5 Viewpoints About Soul Mates," author Barrie Dolnick suggests people not panic if they feel as though they've missed their one shot at "the one." "Soul mates are not a one-shot deal," she states. "Soul mates find you if you are open to them." She also reminds us that soul mates are not permanent and that we need to stop believing in the fairytale ending of finding our life mate and living happily ever after. Even if we were lucky enough to find that twin flame, or perfect soul mate, challenges would continue until death do us part, and beyond! Romances go bad and "soul mates" turn into "sour mates."

This means we have choices, even if we are destined to meet the people we will make those choices with or about. We can choose to get involved with someone, on any level, and choose to stay involved if the relationship goes sour, or we can choose to leave with love and go onto our next soul mate adventure. We are not powerless, or hopeless, or helpless, when it comes to love.

I had the wonderful pleasure of talking to two amazing women who know all about love, finding the One, and how we have choices.

Arielle Ford (www.arielleford.com) is an amazing woman who found her own soul mate at the age of 44. She is a leading pioneer in the personal growth/spirituality movement, is the author of many books, including the best-selling The Soulmate Secret, and helped launch the careers of notables like Dr. Wayne Dyer, Dean Ornish, Jack Canfield, Deepak Chopra, and Louise Hay as a book publicist. Arielle's book and Soulmate Kit are helping people all over the world open their hearts to meeting the One, and her phone interview with me revealed insights that help us realize how much choice we do have in fulfilling the destinies of our hearts. Arielle tells us we need to prepare our bodies, minds, hearts, and even our homes for love to move into our lives, for our perfect partner to arrive at last: "Some of our relationships can be predestined, but again it is our choice as to whether we participate in that relationship and learn from it.... Some of it is pre-destined, but we have choices about all of it. We have free will and a lot of it depends on your level of consciousness."

Arielle also tells us that soul mates can come and go, each one teaching us and helping us to evolve and grow. Some will push our buttons, others will teach, others will heal: "They can be our greatest joy and our biggest heartbreak."

Her keys to helping manifest our soul mate? "You have to create a vacuum, to let people or new experiences in. Most people are too afraid to trust and let go, so they suffer." She also reminds us to look for signs in the universe, and follow those signs, and to keep present moment awareness, staying grateful for where we are now: "Trust yourself to co-create with the universe." And, believing and knowing that the person who is perfect for you is ready for you, knowing they are out there, and acting as if they are already in your life will help the law of attraction do its magic.

That is the key. There can be many people who are perfect for you, because to Arielle, a soul mate is "simply someone who you can be yourself with, and when you look into their eyes you feel like you are home."

Lisa Steadman (www.lisasteadman.com), best-selling author, speaker, coach, and CEO of Woohoo, Inc., has dedicated her life to coaching and empowering people to shine in the world, find love and happiness, and be more of who they were meant to be. She and I spoke about this idea of "the One." She personally did not believe there is just one "One," and that the person sitting next to you on the bus or in line at Starbucks could be the One, because "There is no perfect person, but there is a person who is perfect for you, many of them in fact...."

Lisa suggests making a list of what we seek in a mate, then tearing it up and going for a "feeling" about what we want, rather than a checklist. We also need to re-create our love vocabulary and not be defined by the past: "We create our destiny every day. There can and should be more than one 'One' because we don't usually get it right the first time." Attraction, she reminds us, doesn't always equal compatibility, and often the person we are most drawn to is the worst for us. "Trash the romance movies and novels about destiny and the perfect One, those are fairy tales," she says.

"Thinking that there is a destined person for you can lead to all kinds of anxiety and depression, because you feel like what if you miss that chance meeting...it can make you miserable." Instead, Lisa says to go for being happy rather than looking for a particular label, and that means choosing wisely. There are many Ones out there to choose from!

So there is both a sense of destiny, but plenty of choice, involved in love and friendships. And let's face it, other than money and career, love is the most important thing to us, and we think about it the most (yes, men do, too; don't deny it!). The idea that we are powerless to the choices made before birth, even if our own souls did make them, leaves us feeling as though we may never love and be loved. But wisdom from those in the know tells us we do have choices, and there may even be a little science behind those choices.

In their book, *Attached: The New Science of Adult Attachment and How It Can Help You Find—and Keep—Love*, authors Amir Levine, MD, and Rachel S.F. Heller, MA, found that we all have a particular attachment style that we can learn about and understand. Once we do this, we can make better choices about who we get involved in and how our relationships progress, rather than leaving it all up to chance, or fate.

These attachment styles are evident in our childhood, in how we attached to our primary caretakers, usually our mothers, and are later reflected in how we approach adult relating. The actual attachment styles were discovered by American psychologist Mary Ainsworth, collaborating with British research John Bowlby, the actual founder of "attachment theory." They found three distinct styles that babies and toddlers use to form attachments: secure, anxious, and avoidant. There is a fourth style, but it is much less common. Secure attachments are stable and confident, with the child seeing the mother as a secure base from which to venture forth and explore the world. Those with anxious styles are insecure and preoccupied, even fearful, and tend to be more clingy and needy. Those who are avoidant do just that, avoiding real relating and being detached from emotional needs, constantly trying to minimize their need to be close to anyone. The fourth style is a mixture of anxious and avoidant.

What these attachment styles do is allow us self-discovery, and when we are equipped with knowing what our particular style is, we can then choose better and end up with more satisfying results. Even if we had a less-than-desirable attachment to our primary caregivers, the power is still with us to redesign how we deal with it now, as adults. We can make better choices.

What's Your Calling?

Although we may seek that perfect love, and the friendships and relationships we feel we were destined to have, the same dilemma faces us with the "other" most important aspect of our lives: career, calling, vocation—purpose. Were we put here with a grand purpose in mind, a calling that, should we heed it, will lead us to our destiny? Is leading a life of purpose something that requires we are born with that purpose as a pre-set button that, when pressed, we are compelled to follow?

We have gifts and talents, many of which we are born with, some of which are learned over time. We have things we love to do, and things we could care less spend time on. We have jobs that make us feel fulfilled, and jobs that just pay the bills. Carolyn Myss, author of *Sacred Contracts: Awakening Your Divine Potential*, writes that we come into this life with a contract that, if we follow, will lead us to our divine purpose. We find this purpose through emotional and spiritual growth and our relationships, and by listening to and committing to the Divine within us. As we come to understand ourselves more, and heal emotional wounds of the past, we move closer to that divine purpose. We fulfill our sacred contract.

But we still have a choice, because if we choose not to awaken our divine potential, and follow where that potential leads, we will not reach our divine purpose. We will no doubt live a life that feels off, wrong, as if a constant struggle against the flow of a powerful river. Being on purpose doesn't guarantee there won't be rough spots in life, but often makes the river ride a lot smoother, because we are going with the flow of our destiny.

I can vouch for this, being one of the "lucky" few people out there who knew at a very early age what I was destined to be: a writer. (I wanted to be a jockey, too, but outgrew that desire, figuratively and literally!) I can vouch for how difficult life would get each and every time I forgot my destiny, or got scared, or doubted, and deviated from my path. I paid the price for it with suffering, misery, and depression, not to mention a sense of taking two steps forward, nine steps back. Being in the flow of a purpose that is aligned with your sense of destiny is a powerful and wonderful thing, opening invisible doors where none existed before.

Still, what do you do if you don't know your purpose and feel no discernable pull toward anything other than day-to-day survival? If you don't have a life mission, maybe it's just that you don't remember it, or have lost touch with it. Often we are told to, as Myss says, become more fluent in the language of symbols and archetypes, and pay closer attention to the little intuitions, inspirations, and coincidences that cross our paths. We can even make a "chart of origin," which Myss outlines in her book, and get a profile of our spiritual DNA.

A sense of purpose, or destiny, doesn't have to be huge and involve becoming rich and famous or leading a nation toward peace. We can have smaller purposes that are just as important to our soul's development, and again we can have a different purpose for each incarnation, all leading up to the grand purpose of existence, which as we saw in previous chapters could involve achieving oneness with all that is, and never having to come back here and do it all over again.

But for *this* life, finding one's purpose or calling really may just be a matter of getting quiet enough, and thus slowing down long enough, to hear the inner urgings of our soul. Asking ourselves simple questions such as "Who am I?" and "Why do I feel I am here on earth?" could lead to some amazing answers that propel us forward to a destiny we had been ignoring or suppressing. Yet, how often do we really stop to seriously consider those questions? Not when we have to get on Facebook and check our status, update our Twitter, and watch reality shows. Distractions abound, yet we end up spending most of our lives in a state of ongoing, underlying malaise because we don't feel like we are doing what we were meant to do.

Myss, in *Sacred Contracts*, does suggest getting to know the many archetypes that provide us with our life lessons and challenges, and teaches how we can work with them to achieve our personal and divine goals. For those who shy away from the more metaphysical approaches to destiny and calling, it might just be a matter of going back to those college career counseling days and asking yourself what you are good at, what you like to do, and what others say you excel at, and take it from there.

Sometimes, a calling is not about job or work, but about a way of being in the world, living as an example to others. Whether through non-profit work, volunteering, or just "going green," people who are finding their callings don't have to require that they quit their jobs to pursue the watercolor painting they loved as a kid. It doesn't have to be that hard. But if, after a great deal of meditation and thought, you realize your calling *is* watercolor painting, then does it not behoove you to go for it? In a quotation attributed to Johann Wolfgang von Goethe (though no one source has ever actually been found; it appears to be a hodgepodge of quotes from various people), "The moment one definitely commits oneself, then Providence moves as well. All sorts of things occur to help one that would never otherwise have occurred. A stream of events issues from the decision, raising in one's favor all manner of unforeseen accidents, meetings, and material assistance that no one could have dreamed would come their way. Whatever you can do or dream you can do, begin it. Boldness has genius, power and magic in it. Begin it now."

We might replace the word *providence* with *destiny*, for those who truly follow their calling believe with every fiber of their being that they are moving toward a destiny that is theirs and theirs alone. They make choices all along the way, but if they stay on course, the actions of providence will push them along to the end result, making each step of life a bit easier and less of a struggle.

In his book, *Transforming Fate Into Destiny: A New Dialogue With Your Soul,"* renowned intuitive and teacher Robert Ohotto talks about the "Heroic Journey of the Soul," which suggests that the challenges and obstacles we face are the keys to the unlived life we seek. The "psychic energy" from our family patterns and cultural beliefs, and even global evolution all play a role in what we are each "Fated" with, and the cards we are dealt. We, though, do the work of uniting what Ohotto sees as the two forces of the universe, Fate, and destiny, to move toward our ultimate purpose. We become the heros and heroines of our own lives. He tells us: "Destiny is your capacity to live out the threads of your Fate in a unique way that only you can do, while having a positive vibrational impact on the world's energy and soul."

Ohotto believes our souls make two contracts before birth: an agreement with Fate, which consists of our mortal limitations, and our agreement with destiny, which allows us to alchemically transform our Fate and all of its challenges into the gold of a soul-directed life: "Transforming Fate into Destiny is the process of becoming your authentic self so that you manifest the mystery of creation, actively embodying purpose, joy and meaning."

The book also suggests watching for the hurdles and challenges that keep cropping up in your life, as indicators of lessons not yet learned. I often think the universe hands us a lesson gently the first time, and if we don't get it then, the second, third, and fourth times will be a lot more painful. So why not try to get it the first time? Even breaking the spells of old beliefs and traditions that no longer serve us is a necessity to clearing the path of destiny. If we live our lives thinking and believing what others tell us to, we never even know our authentic selves enough to identify our purpose to begin with.

The great thing is, our purpose can end up being as simple or as grand as raising children who are loving and caring, building a community garden that will live on long after we do, or writing a best-selling book that changes lives. It is about what *our* purpose is, and not what we think it should be. Other people's purposes are their own, and not a barometer against which we should measure ours. My destiny is mine, and yours is yours. My choices are also mine. Yours are yours. That is the path toward true authenticity and discovering our purpose.

According to *Mechthild of Magdeburg: The Flowing Light of the Godhead (Classics of Western Spirituality)*, Mechthild of Magdeburg, a Medieval mystic, once said, "A fish cannot drown in water. A bird does not fall in air. Each creature God made must live in its own true nature." Rest assured, you don't have to find your purpose when you are any specific age. As Oprah Winfrey states in *What I Know For Sure*, we are *all* called, and if we are still breathing, we still have a contribution to make. "There is no greater gift," she writes, "you can give or receive than to honor your calling. It's why you were born. And how you become most truly alive."

Soul Groups and Life Lessons:
Destiny, Fate, and Free Will From a Spiritual Perspective
by Sherry Hopson

Expansion and creation are the energetic forces that drive our universe. As creatures of this universe it is the inherent nature of human souls to continually expand and create. We are driven to expand our consciousness along many paths, and destiny is simply the endpoint of any one of those paths. Within this pathway is the life pathway, the soul group pathway and the karmic pathway. When all three have reached the same frequency and vibration, the destiny of the soul current path has occurred. Each pathway contains lessons for the soul to learn and to achieve. The soul exists in more than one soul group at a time and may have more than destiny it is striving to achieve.

We walk these paths with others who share similar aspirations, our soul group. Members of a soul group have chosen at the spiritual level, before incarnation, to learn a set of lessons through experiences as living beings. When those lessons have been learned, the belief system of the physical person has been changed, and the vibratory frequency of the individual's soul has been raised. The being ceases membership in that soul group and joins another to learn different lessons and achieve other destinies.

Take the example of Joe, who derives his self-worth from his work. Joe focuses his creative energy on his work. Joe is a member of many soul groups, but we'll consider just one. The individuals in this group are learning how to balance energy across several areas of existence, rather than focusing it on one. The lesson they are here to learn is balance.

Joe's experience of his current life is that it's all about work. He thinks nothing of working 60 hours a week, because it makes his self-worth soar and his body buzz with energy. The concerns of his family come last.

If something isn't directly related to helping him do his job, Joe's belief system says it isn't important. Healthy eating, giving emotionally to his wife or kids, trips to the doctor, vacations, hobbies—none of these are on Joe's agenda. In his belief system, they would take energy away from where he gets his creative "charge" and his self-worth: his work.

However, in the minds of everyone else who comes into contact with him, Joe needs to "get a life."

So the universe helps Joe along by giving him a gentle wake-up: It makes him sick. Stress, lack of sleep, improper eating, and lack of human connections all have taken their toll on Joe. His illness is a result of unbalanced living. It is his own creation in interaction with his environment, not something imposed upon him solely from without.

Here is where free will comes into play: Joe can choose to take advantage of the learning opportunity afforded by his illness. He can put balance into his life and use his creative energy in other areas—for example, in parenting, and derive more of his self worth from being "Daddy."

Joe can choose to ask himself why the illness came when it did: what he was doing that contributed to getting sick—taking responsibility for his creation—or how he could change his behavior to ensure that it doesn't happen again. But in this case Joe chooses to regard his illness as nothing more than a random "bug" that stops him from achieving work goals and keeps him from the emotional high that his work gives him. He doesn't see it as anything for which he is responsible. He refuses to rest and finally he drags himself back to work, still sick. Lesson not learned.

Joe throws his energy even more completely into his work to make up for the time he missed. The universe now provides Joe with another opportunity to learn balance, but this time it does so more forcefully. Joe mistakenly presses "reply to all" instead of "reply" when he sends out an e-mail critical of an employee. This brings the energy of the entire work group down, and eventually the project team that Joe wants to join hires someone else.

To Joe, this knock to his self-worth is like getting hit with a 2x4. He throws himself even more into his work, now spending 80 hours a week attempting to get the same emotional high he was used to. Again he fails to consider his contribution to the situation. Instead, he blames the project team. And again, lesson not learned.

With each failed opportunity to learn, the energy associated with this lesson accumulates in Joe's life, like a buildup of static electricity. Eventually it becomes so strong that it discharges with serious consequences. That is fate stepping in.

While driving home from work late one rainy night, Joe is stewing over the slight from the project team. He rushes a red light and ends up in a serious car accident, for which he is at fault. The company is sued. Joe loses his job and nearly his life. In the painful months that follow, while he is bedridden and cannot work, Joe has no other choice but to learn to balance his life differently. If he fails to do this, he would simply have no self-worth at all.

Was this fate? Yes. Did Joe exercise free will? Yes. Joe had the free will—the choice—to see each incident as an opportunity to learn the lesson of balance. Had he learned that lesson early in the process, the consequences would have been less extreme. But because Joe freely chose not to learn the lesson when each opportunity was presented, the energy to follow his karmic path (which I am calling "fate") built until it was unavoidable.

It is our destiny to learn the lesson of our soul group. It is our free will to choose the point along the path where we will learn that lesson. A lesson can be deferred, but it cannot be denied. And the longer we take to learn it, the greater the build-up of karmic energy about it—our fate. Eventually the lesson will be learned. Once it is learned, our belief system changes, and so, in turn, does the frequency of our spiritual vibration.

—Sherry Hopson (www.sherryhopson.com) is an internationally known psychic counselor specializing in soul memories and soul paths.

There will always be those who ascribe it all to luck. Lucky are those who pick the winning lottery numbers, who are born gorgeous, or who find that perfect love match. Luck, though, is actually something we can work on by choice, and may have nothing to do with our destiny (although if we are following our destiny, we most likely will feel lucky because we are on purpose!). Luck is positive attraction, and we can all find ways to increase our chances of being in the right place at the right time should opportunity come knocking.

In an article for *Women's Health* magazine titled "Make Your Own Luck," we learn of scientific studies done at University of Hertfordshire by psychologist Richard Wiseman, PhD. Wiseman, who is also the author of *The Luck Factor*, found after a decade of research that only about 10 percent of life is random or pure chance: "The rest is luck, and luck is determined by your attitude towards life, by what you put out into the universe and how you respond to the results." Some of the ways he suggests increasing your luck include literally considering yourself lucky. People who do this actually tend to be luckier, because it is a self-fulfilling prophecy. Shifting one's focus can also open up opportunities we never saw before. Of course, he suggests taking more risks and breaking familiar patterns as well, as both tend to keep us living in a small box, our comfort zone, and luck often comes to those who are willing to step out of the box. This is aligned with popular law of attraction teachings that tell us to focus our thought, intention, and action on what we want, not on what we don't want. The energy we put out is what we get back, and if we feel lucky and blessed, we will bring more of that feeling back to us in the form of more things to feel lucky and blessed about.

Regardless, this shows that we have numerous input, control, and choices to play with even if we do believe we have an ultimate destiny, or end point. It's like deciding to go to Hawaii. You can swim there, fly there, ride there on the back of a whale, and take any number of routes and detours to get there. Ultimately you desire to get to the Big Island. That is your destiny.

Why then, if we have all these choices, and a true purpose to strive toward, are so many people miserable and depressed and filled with worry? Millions of people walk the earth believing they are only alive for a specific duration of time, and that what happens to them is out of their control at most, and what they can control is minimal. This is an extreme way to look at both destiny and choice as the foundation for a purpose-filled life. Instead, why not choose to look at your life as a gift you were given, some of it planned out at a higher level, with choice available to you all along the duration of the time you will walk this planet, that can either lead you to your destiny or at the very least provide you with lessons that must be learned regardless? Tossing a life off to pure luck or chance is one extreme. Feeling as though you have to control every aspect and that it is all in the choices you make as you go along, is another extreme.

The truth most likely sits on the fence in the middle—and knows.

Conclusion

Straddling the Fence: Destiny and Choice

"I seldom end up where I want to go, but almost always end up where I need to be."
—Douglas Adams

"The willing, Destiny guides them. The unwilling, Destiny drags them."
—Seneca

Arizona State University cosmologist Paul Davies will utilize grant money from the Foundational Questions Institute (*www.fqxi. org*) to try to determine the destiny of the universe. Using a radical reformulation of quantum mechanics, Davies hopes to find out if the universe has a distinct destiny, a fate of its own, as well as if the future of the universe can reach back in influence the past. Working off of earlier attempts by physicist Yakir Aharanov, who argued that, although the workings of the universe appeared random, there was in fact hidden order, Davies will look to find his own workable theory of how the future might influence the past, thus requiring a quantum leap in our understanding of causality and our traditional views of time.

The quantum world tells us that all is potentiality at first, until observed into a fixed state. If that is true, then Fate is one hell of a micro-manager. Can you imagine all of the possible predestined futures that exist in the quantum foamy sea of all possibility—each of those futures with a distinct path and outcome? Each with a determined set of sign posts along the way?

Yet someone, or something, has to choose from among those potentialities and pick the one that will become the reality, at least in *this* universe.

On January 6, 2011, the Pope came out with a bold statement that God was behind the Big Bang, and that the universe was not an accident. Reuters reporter Phillip Pullelia wrote for Yahoo! News that the Pope believed God's mind was behind the complex scientific theories of the Big Bang, and that "[t]he universe is not the result of chance, as some would want to make us believe." The Catholic Church doesn't teach creationism anymore, accepting evolution as scientific theory that does not have to be out of alignment with God. In fact, God uses the evolutionary process to form the human species, suggesting an evolving God.

All else is allegory, the Pope says.

So religion and science both theorize that the universe—our cosmos—had a beginning and a purpose and a destiny, and one day it will all end. How and when we are still awash in theory about. But suffice it to say, more and more people are accepting a sense of predestination when it comes to our universe and ourselves—even as we continue to make choices as to how we arrive at that destination.

Shorty after the Pope's stunning admission, an article appeared in Yahoo! News about a Texas man named Cornelius Dupree, Jr., who spent 30 years in a Texas prison for a crime he never committed. Dupree, Jr. was exonerated only after DNA evidence showed his innocence, but he can never get back those 30 years, can he? DNA tells everything: who we are, what we are, even who did what to whom. Was it this man's destiny to be imprisoned on false charges, or was it the random choices of those who accused and convicted him? How ironic that DNA evidence would set him free.

Writing this book ended up being far more difficult than I first imagined. What I had thought would be a slam dunk for one or the other, looking at all the circumstantial evidence (and I call it that because we don't really know for sure) for both destiny and choice made me realize I had stumbled into a rabbit hole that went on forever and ever. In fact, this rabbit hole had no bottom, because First Cause was the bottom, and we are still chasing that elusive mystery. Until we find it, we will continue falling.

Much of my own life has smacked of destiny, from knowing what I was going to do from a very early age (write) to many of the amazing synchronicities and miracles that got me from point A to point B. And yet, I also made choices. Good choices. Bad choices. Stupid choices! When the choices did not align with the destined path, I felt it in the way of blocked goals, miserable relationships, poor health, and general malaise that seemingly went away once I got back "on track."

I could argue with you readers until we are all blue in the face that destiny is real and that choice is how we get there, if we get there, but no matter how valid my arguments, and no matter how good my "evidence" looks, the truth is, you won't be moved until and unless you experience it all for yourselves. Everyone has their own tales to tell about how they feel aspects of their lives were destined, planned, and purposeful, and also those times in their lives when a choice made all the difference in how things turned out. Whether or not it was all, in reality, pre-planned, or all a total crapshoot, most of us just cannot say with absolute certainty. We go on what we feel. We go on experience.

We go on faith.

Social networking is huge, and I admit to partaking in it daily, despite my mile-high goal list. But it serves a purpose. I learn things. Being on Facebook and watching the dramas and tragedies and love and success stories played out right before my eyes, seeing some people have their dreams fulfilled, and others losing what they most held dear, made me realize that we long for a sense of destiny. The word may be romanticized, because what we really want is to feel like whatever made us did so with a tiny bit of thought and concern as to our welfare. We want to believe we count, we matter, we have a purpose, no matter how big or small, and that we aren't just little wads of biochemical mush thrown out into the wind to blow at random. If something good happens, we want to believe it was "meant to be" and if something awful occurs, we want to hope that it is our "life lesson"; nothing is purely random.

And yet, we long for freedom to choose, and the power of choice. We want to feel like we matter and have some say over the course of our lives. We want to feel powerful, effective, and decisive—until something awful happens, and then we seemingly revert back into a child seeking a parent to explain the "why?"

I watched in wonder on Facebook one day as one family waited to hear about whether or not a newborn would live; he did not. Meanwhile, another friend waited to hear the diagnosis of a biopsy; it was benign. I had to ask myself: Was the first family destined to lose a baby? And was the friend destined to be healthy and cancer-free? Was all of this planned ahead of time, before any of the players were even born? Were they fully in charge of what was happening in their lives?

Was I?

Destiny allows us to accept a tragedy, or a success, and give it a meaning so that we don't go insane with the thought that it is all beyond our control, and we mean nothing at all in a larger sense. If we lose a baby, we can say that it was destined, for that baby was meant to teach us a lesson here about love and loss, and move on quickly to its next incarnation. If we survive an illness, we say it was meant to be as we learned a great life lesson and the illness transformed us. We simply cannot live with a belief that these things happen *at random*, and we are nothing more than moving targets hoping we don't get hit on any given day of the week.

It couldn't be choice, could it? For someone to choose to lose a child or spouse, or get ovarian or breast or throat cancer—it *has* to be part of a bigger puzzle, the pieces of which we just don't have all of yet. For to be pure choice also means we are at the mercy of our own monkey minds, unable to make the best choices—manifesting at random out of the murk of the subconscious. So we give ourselves the belief in destiny when something happens, and then we make the choices as to how we react and deal with that destined event. Therein lies the balance.

Shit happens, but we choose how to deal with it.

Destiny is our desire to matter in the greater scheme of things. Choice is our desire to feel like we are doing the driving—even if the car is under the ultimate control of someone, or something, else. Destiny is why we are here, and choice is how we plan to live the life we were given.

Think of going to the store and buying a brand-new jigsaw puzzle. It comes in a box, and on the cover is an image of the completed puzzle. The bigger picture, so to speak. Life is the puzzle, and perhaps destiny is the bigger picture that, when finished, we can sit back and feel a sense of completion about. Yet we still have the choice to open the box and begin the long and often arduous process of putting together all those pieces, many of which look exactly alike. Some people just don't have the patience, or the ability, to look beyond the singular pieces to the overall end result. Maybe choice is nothing more than a series of singular pieces we can, or cannot, work in place to get to that desired end result.

In the end, we straddle the fence, listening for intuitive guidance, watching for signs along the path of life that point the way, and all the while choosing to either listen and follow, or ignore and go the other direction. On one side of the fence we find purpose, meaning, and a sense of predetermined fate. On the other, free will calls with the lure of the open road and potentialities galore. On one side, we see a cosmic destiny from the birth to the death of our universe, with finely tuned laws and ratios at work along the way pointing to evolutionary developments that eventually led to life. On the other, we as human beings exercise choice in everyday life the way we exercise our bodies. It comes naturally to us to believe we have a say in the schemes of our own existence.

On one side of the fence, DNA and genetics tell us we will be blond and blue-eyed, or tall and lean. On the other side, we choose to eat ourselves into obesity, or work out like demons and look like *Jersey Shore*'s The Situation on steroids.

On one side of the fence, we are born, we age, and we die, and nothing we do can stop that train. Slow it down a bit, maybe. But we can't stop the Destiny Train of a single human life. On the other side of the fence, we can choose to live a full life in only 20 years, or an empty life in 97. It's up to us how we use the time we get.

This book has been a wild, wild ride, bringing up for me personal issues of both fate and choice, as I looked back over my own life and saw the puzzle pieces that fell together as if predestined to do so—and the ones I tried my mightiest to force into place even though they didn't fit. The trajectory of my life has been a fine blend of the two, with more on the side of destiny, simply because, at my age, with all my experience I can now truly say I am listening to my inner voice, letting it guide me, and trying to stay focused on my goals. And when I do, I am happier and "feel" more as if my life has meaning, purpose, and power.

As if I have a destiny.

Maybe as we grow older, we come to realize that the power of our choices creates our character, and thus our destiny. Few of us feel like we were born to do or be a specific something, and for those who do, more power to them. They are lucky to know their destiny from such an early age. But for the rest of us, there is an underlying sense of exploration and discovery, that maybe when we get a few more years under our belts we will finally figure out who we are and why we are here. We won't find our destiny so much as we will finally let it find us. We will give up the resistance and struggle, the fears and doubts and insecurities that keep us from moving boldly toward our dreams, no matter what those dreams may be.

A life, no matter how long it lasts, is someone's choice—our parents, their parents before them, and theirs before them. Think about it: Your existence on this earth began as far back as the first moment in time, because if you back-engineer the choices that led up to your existence, you will have to go all the way back to First Cause. Your parents were the choice of their parents, and so on and so on, and you would not be here if somewhere along the way there was a break in the chain.

Is that one big, long chain of choice? Or of destiny?

If it goes all the way back to First Cause, then each and every one of us was planned, predestined, predetermined, even if it was in the most indirect of ways imaginable.

On one side of the fence, each of us—you—were meant to be. On the other side of the fence, two people had to have sex to conceive you, and that was an act of choice.

Either way, you are here, and you now have the choice to make your life what you were destined to, because, in the end, no matter what side of the fence you are focusing on, the fence stays the same.

A *hung jury*, according to legal dictionaries, is a term that is used when a trial jury is unable to reach a unanimous or near-unanimous verdict. This means jurors are unable to determine, as a collective body, whether or not a defendant is guilty or not guilty, or in a civil case that a jury was unable to find for the plaintiff or for the defendant.

As I conclude this book, I would have to say that when it comes to the battle between destiny and choice, in a court of law most likely there would be a hung jury. That is because so much of the evidence presented is by nature circumstantial. Circumstantial evidence is any information and testimony presented that permit conclusions that indirectly establish the existence or nonexistence of a fact or event that the party seeks to prove. It is also known as "indirect evidence." According to the *Free Online Law Dictionary* it is

> distinguished from direct evidence, which, if believed, proves the existence of a particular fact without any inference or presumption required. Circumstantial evidence relates to a series of facts other than the particular fact sought to be proved. The party offering circumstantial evidence argues that this series of facts, by reason and experience, is so closely associated with the fact to be proved that the fact to be proved may be inferred simply from the existence of the circumstantial evidence.

Science, whether we are talking the creation of the cosmos and the universe we live in, or the genetic background that makes us human, leans more in the direction of destiny. We have no say in the creation of galaxies, and we have no say in the DNA that makes us blonde or tall or bald or small. There is, in the scientific world, a true sense of predestined outcomes that are far outside the realm of our control.

When it comes to our individual lives, though, we lean toward more choice and free will. We can decide whom to mate with, and thus determine the genetic makeup of our own offspring (to a small extent!), and we can choose our jobs, where we live, and whether or not we run that marathon next year. There still may be a strong sense of purpose, direction, and destiny to our lives, but we still feel we have choices.

Either way, we still end up with a hung jury because, as factual and direct as all the evidence may seem, without knowing what started this all leaves us with no perpetrator, and no motive. Only if we know what First Cause is, and what it intended by all of this life and existence stuff, do we get the facts (and just the facts, ma'am). Otherwise, it's all circumstantial.

Maybe that's the way it's supposed to be. If we thought our lives were set in stone, we would feel hopeless and without purpose. If we thought it was all up to us, we would feel terrified and inadequate. Striking just the right balance between destiny and choice makes for the best outcome possible, no matter what the First Cause may have been.

A life well lived.

> "Everything is determined, the beginning as well as the end, by forces over which we have no control. It is determined for the insect, as well as for the star. Human beings, vegetables, or cosmic dust, we all dance to a mysterious tune, intoned in the distance by an invisible piper."
> —Albert Einstein

> "Ideals are like stars; you will not succeed in touching them with your hands. But like the seafaring man on the desert of waters, you choose them as your guides, and following them you will reach your destiny."
> —Carl Schurz

> "Experts in ancient Greek culture say that people back then didn't see their thoughts as belonging to them. When ancient Greeks had a thought, it occurred to them as a god or goddess giving an order. Apollo was telling them to be brave. Athena was telling them

to fall in love. Now people hear a commercial for sour cream potato chips and rush out to buy, but now they call this free will. At least the ancient Greeks were being honest."
   —Chuck Palahniuk

Appendix

You Are My Density: Stories of Fate and Free Will

George McFly: Lorraine, my density has bought me to you.

Lorraine Baines: What?

George McFly: Oh, what I meant to say was...

Lorraine Baines: Wait a minute, don't I know you from somewhere?

George McFly: Yes. Yes. I'm George, George McFly. I'm your density. I mean...your destiny.

—Back to the Future, 1985

In the hugely popular time travel movie *Back to the Future*, a young man named Marty McFly travels back in time to 1955 to make sure his future parents meet, kiss, and fall in love. Otherwise, he's toast—and he will never be conceived or born. In one scene, in a coffee shop, the nerdy George McFly, Marty's future father, is trying to find the courage to talk to the popular Lorraine, who will become Marty's mother. Marty himself is coaching George to find his inner lion and go talk to the girl. Interestingly, the girl, Lorraine, has the hots for Marty, not knowing he is her own son who has come back to the past.

Eventually, George overcomes his fear and proclaims his love for Lorraine by misreading from his notepad, "You are my density." He is met with a puzzled look by Lorraine, forcing him to re-read his notes and correct himself with "You are my destiny." They eventually kiss, get it on, and have Marty. Truly this is a love story about destiny, and brings up the very important point of what happens if one aspect of the past is altered, thus altering one's destiny.

Still, it's just a movie. But it rang true on so many levels with audiences, and still does to this day. Imagine how many marriage proposals begin with the humorous mis-wording: You are my density.

We love stories like this.

The following are stories and insights from real people from all walks of life who have experienced the pull of destiny, or the power of choice, in their own lives. I like to feature real stories like this because, aside from the facts and theories and ideas presented in this book, when we see how destiny and choice worked in others lives, it often awakens us to the realization of how destiny and choice have been at work in our own. Enjoy the stories and be inspired by the ways that we all seem to end up where we need to be.

Determinism vs. Free Will?
By Scott Westmoreland

It seems to me that the question of whether life is predetermined or entirely free will is the wrong question, much as the notion of having an inside, without an outside, or a back without a front. You can't have one without the other. They are opposite, and yet the same. So, my answer is both, at once. Imagine you are on a cruise ship, and you are destined for Acapulco—that's what your ticket says. Now, during the ride, you are free to indulge in whatever activities you wish. You can chose your meals, whom you spend your time with, what activities you wish to partake in, even which way you are facing (forward or backward). The ship's ultimate course acts independent of your good or bad opinion of it (kinda like the shape and color of your eyes, or the age in which your hair might start falling out!?). Now, you will naturally have a sense of whether or not you are making the journey smoothly or naturally by your personal choices. You will surely notice if you stick a paddle in the ocean and try to force your will to change the ship's course, but ultimately, you are constantly still on board, and bound for a prearranged destination.

Perhaps you even consulted with the captain prior to deciding to make the journey (wink-wink).

Another analogy came to me in a dream state vision. I was placed at the perspective of being high above a body of water, which flowed gently and naturally from right to left and ultimately funneled in to a larger body of water. As I navigated through life, I could see myself rowing smoothly with the current in to tranquil waters near the left. Then I could see myself turning and heading right (upstream), struggling against the natural flow, toward turbulence. Finally, I was shown where I currently sat within the river. As the witness to it all, still safely observing from above, I had to chuckle at this poor guy down below. He was always safe, always protected in this water. If he just stopped efforting, the natural course of the current was gonna get him to his predetermined destination!

So, have we not all had times in our lives when, despite our most heroic efforts—when an outcome seemed like a "slam dunk"—we still didn't have things go our way!? Or, times when something seemed absolutely impossible, and the universe just magically "lined up" and we experienced the miraculous! We utter, "Man, I couldn't have written this script!?" These are examples of how the two worlds collide. Learn to merge the dichotomy, and let go of the outcomes. Embrace the unknown and life will be the exciting and unpredictable ride you prearranged it to be.

Scott Westmoreland has been a professional entertainer, writer, and fine artist. His already-amazing life was enhanced greatly as an adult following only what he describes as an instantaneous and colossal "spiritual awakening." This has lead to deep interests in the works left for us by the likes of Walter Russell, Alan Watts, Deepak Chopra, and many others, as well as validating discoveries in the field of Quantum Physics. For more information, please visit www.scottwestmorelandart.com.

Free Will or Destiny?
By Cindy Pacheco

If you've seen the movie *The Proposal*, you've seen a snippet of my life, having married someone who is not a U.S.-born citizen. Was it destiny? If it is, then I've been dragged into it kicking and screaming. Was it free will? That's what I'd like to think. Still, if there wasn't something bigger than free will keeping me in this relationship I might have left a long time ago.

After a whirlwind two-month "courtship" I married my teacher.

It's interesting how I came to be in his class. At the last minute, early in the semester, I dropped a class and added another. Not an extraordinary event for many, but rare for me.

My new cartography teacher was a "foreigner." In 1988 we didn't have many Asians in my little town, and I couldn't decide if he was Mexican or Chinese. He was young and energetic and seemed pretty darn fearless, standing in front the classroom, teaching confidently in his heavily accented English. I admired his bravery.

Studious as Hermione Grainger, I spent most of my spring break that semester in the cartography lab working on a project for his class. None of my classmates seemed to have shared my enthusiasm for drawing with pen and ink and making pretty maps, as I was the only one in the lab except for my teaching assistant.

We talked for hours as I bent over my work. He was good-natured and talkative, and I learned he was Filipino. I found him pleasant company. Sweet and attentive, though not particularly handsome, he soon charmed me anyway and we started dating—very discreetly. Student/teacher relationships weren't exactly condoned by the university. At the end of the semester, we attended a fancy reception given by the department of geography and to our amazement both our names were called at the awards ceremony. We received the outstanding teaching assistant and outstanding student awards for the department!

Soon after the semester ended he was offered a job in Chicago. He asked me to marry him and I said, "No." He was persistent, however, and 22 years later we're still together. The stories I could tell about the challenges of blending two very different sets of cultural values would amaze and confuse most people. I suppose I thrive on challenge. We have a wonderful daughter now and the world is a better place with her in it, so it may well have been destiny after all.

Next Stop: The Destiny Zone
By Julia K. Cole

I've always known my purpose was helping others. What I didn't know, until much later in life, was that this purpose had a particular way of being fulfilled, leaving no room for compromise. During my early adult life, I avoided being who I am, doing what I do because I wanted to fit in—to be normal. To be like everybody else! The last thing I wanted to be was a psychic medium!

In the early 1990s I worked at a local radio station where I met a psychic from Dallas, Texas, who was making her annual guest appearance on our morning show. She and I came face-to-face in the hallway outside the control booth that day during a commercial break. Grabbing my arm, she said, "Your granny told me about you. You got a job to do and like it or not, you're gonna do it! No more hiding! No more pretending, sugar!" Of course, I responded by saying "I don't know what you're talking about" and walked away.

She was only one of literally hundreds who had given me a similar message over the years. This time, however, it took on a different feeling, one I couldn't easily shrug off. Two months later, I left the station to work at a law firm. It wasn't long before my boss was asking me, "Why are you hiding?" Though I was good at my job, he somehow knew I didn't fit in. He encouraged me to follow my heart—to be who I really was and stop pretending. He then gave me a business card. Blood rushed to my face as I read the name. It was the psychic woman from Dallas, Texas! Naturally, timing being what it is, she was in town.

I made my appointment and begrudgingly went to her hotel room that evening. I didn't want to be there, but I couldn't find the strength to leave. Sitting across from one another, saying nothing for what seem like an eternity, she broke the silence by asking, "Aren't you tired of all this pretending? You know what you're here to do. Why are you fighting it so much?"

To my own utter amazement I found myself screaming, "I give up! All right? I give up!" Leaning back, smiling, she replied, "Then let's get busy!" The rest—as they say—is history!

Julia K. Cole is a psychic medium, life coach, Internet radio talk show host, and avid duct tape enthusiast and collector.

Fig. 9A

Callea Sherrill standing outside the Carriage House of the Stanley Hotel.

From Hobby to Passion
By Callea Sherrill

As a teenager, I lived in a house with activity, but if you had asked me then if I would grow up and begin looking for paranormal activity for *fun*, I would have thought you were crazy. Then along came a show called *Ghost Hunters*. I knew nothing about the field of paranormal investigations when I began watching it.

One day while Googling information about the show, I came across an event that was taking place at the Stanley Hotel a few weeks later. Having no idea of the popularity of that type of event, I clicked on the link to buy a ticket, only to find it was sold out. Although, this was not something I would normally do, I sent an e-mail to the organizer of the event, asking if he had a waiting list. He informed me that he did indeed have a waiting list, but everyone on it was looking for multiple tickets. He had just heard from a friend who had only 1 ticket, but was unable to attend. The ticket was mine! At that event, not only did I have an incredible experience, but I also met several wonderful people. I was addicted.

Fast-forward to March 2009. My husband was offered a job in Estes Park. He really wanted to take the job, but never imagined I would agree. Surprising even myself, I said, "Let's go!" Since my first experience at the Stanley, I had joined a team in Colorado, and had also traveled across the country to some of the famously haunted locations. The paranormal had become not just a hobby, but a passion.

As soon as we got settled in Estes Park, out of curiosity, I sent an e-mail to the Stanley Hotel asking if they needed a part-time tour guide with experience in the paranormal. Within 24 hours of sending that e-mail, I was interviewed and hired. Since that time, the hotel has developed a new position, based strictly on my talents and knowledge. Neither the management at the hotel, nor I, had imagined how well the partnership would work.

Why do I believe it was destiny? If you had asked me just two years ago, "Would you like to be the resident paranormal investigator at the Stanley Hotel?" my response would have been, "Of course!" But if you had asked me how I could accomplish that goal, I wouldn't have had the slightest idea. Too many obstacles were in the way. And yet, here I am. Exactly where I am supposed to be.

Callea Sherrill is the resident paranormal investigator for the world-famous Stanley Hotel.

A Novel Destiny
By Michelle Griffin

"My density…has brought me to you." It probably doesn't take much to recall that classic line by the character George McFly to Lorraine in the movie *Back to the Future*. I recall wondering, after I finished laughing at poor George's flub, about destiny. Could it really be that our entire lives were already planned out and that, as Shakespeare said, "all the world's a stage and all the men and women merely players"? It was a bit troubling to my fragile ego to consider myself a puppet.

There have been many synchronistic moments in my life that have been so compelling I couldn't help but feel they were destined to occur. In 1993, I was fortunate enough to visit Lily Dale, a spiritualist community in Chautauqua County, New York. I had a wonderful weekend with time spent at Inspiration Stump, open Gallery type readings, and even had a private reading. It was almost time to head home and so I stopped in at the gift shop, wanting to take something symbolic of my time, home with me. I recall a large round table covered in a white tablecloth sitting in the center of the room. On the table was a small pyramid of books. The book was *The Celestine Prophecy* by author James Redfield. I hadn't heard of the book or the author, and wondered why I was drawn to the basic green cover. I picked it up and ran my hand back and forth across the hardback cover. (I've never figured out why I do that, but I can say that I have a real relationship with my books). I wanted this book but it was a little out of college student budget. I looked at the title again, *The Celestine Prophecy*, and decided that it must be about angels and that really wasn't my "thing" so I put it down and chose something else, of which I can not remember.

Fast-forward to late 2002, my dear friend Melissa and I had gotten into the habit of book sharing. We would get together and exchange books we had already finished. One afternoon, Melissa walked in the door with the usual stack of two or three books and held one out to me saying, "I think you'll really like this book." I took it from her and my mouth fell open. I immediately recognized that basic green cover! At that point in my life I had really immersed myself in paranormal investigations and had begun to explore the psychic and spiritual sides of myself as well. I had found my passion and purpose. I told her the story of how I had held that book in Lily Dale almost a decade earlier and even commented that I must be meant to read this book. I thank Melissa for being the deliverer of what felt like destiny.

That evening I sat down and began to read the book that I would find almost impossible to put down. Countless times during reading, I would say out loud, "I knew it!" regarding the spiritual "Insights" presented. Then I would realize that these spiritual ideas were new to me; I couldn't have known these things. I began to wonder, and now believe, that it was my soul resonating with things it already new. I was experiencing what it felt like to hear a divine truth. James Redfield has admitted that, even though he considers the book to be a novel, his intention was to write a story in the shape of a parable, a story meant to illustrate a point or teach a lesson. He accomplished that with me and well more than 20 million other readers.

I think of the day that book came back into my life as the beginning of new, more profound existence. It helped make sense of and validate experiences I had had throughout my life, some which had scared me. One day in 1994, I had had a very heated argument on the phone. When I hung up, I was so enraged that I threw the handset across the room. When the phone had left my hand to begin its assault on a nearby wall, I saw streaks of blue and white emanate from my fingers. It looked a lot like the small flames we see coming from the pilot light of our gas stoves except they extended out about 4 inches from each finger and they had an electric look to them. It scared me deeply, not knowing what it was, and it was well more than a decade before I mentioned it to anyone. When I read the 3rd Insight in *The Celestine Prophecy* I realized that it had been my own built up, angry energy that I saw.

I consider my life to be quite blessed. I have beautiful kids and an adoring husband, and my work is my passion. I own Through The Veil Productions LLC, and I create and host paranormal and metaphysical events, the largest of which happens every June in Atlanta. The past several years, I've been asked many times who my ultimate speaker at one of my events would be. My answer has always been James Redfield. I had written several times over the years in attempts but all to no avail—that is, until this year, 2011. One day my phone rang and I heard a friendly male voice on the other end. I didn't recognize it and asked who was calling. He said, "James. James Redfield." I managed to hold a fairly coherent conversation and was happy that he couldn't see me pacing or see the tears in my eyes.

Unbelievably, as I was rambling and relating the story of Lily Dale and my friend Melissa to James, my call waiting beeped. I knew I wouldn't answer it but was still curious as to who was calling. I looked down at my caller ID and saw a familiar name: Melissa.

So, although I believe in free will and choice, I also believe that there are experiences we are destined to have along the way. Maybe our free will (putting the book down and walking away) sends us in another direction for a while, but sooner or later some things are just destined to happen.

Michelle Griffin is a wife, mother, psychic intuitive, and paranormal investigator residing in Atlanta, Georgia. She is the owner and director of Through The Veil Productions LLC (www.throughtheveil.org), producing premiere paranormal and metaphysical events, the largest of which happens each June in Atlanta.

Could My Childhood Writing Have Led Me to My Destiny?
By Sara Harrison

When I was a little girl, I loved to write stories. On my wedding day in 1990, my mother gave one of those old stories to me. I was shocked at how predictive it was. The story told about a foreign prince who was bearded, was not very tall, and spoke a different language than his girlfriend did. He wanted to take her to his country and make her his bride, but the girl's family had reservations, as the prince had no money whatsoever. Still, love prevailed and the girl married the man, and that was where my story ended.

On the day my mother gave me the story, I was to marry my graduate student boyfriend who was short, was bearded, and had no income to speak of. The most startling aspect was that the prince in my story's name was Theodore, and on that day I married a Canadian man named Theodore. His first language was Slovenian, and he also had a Canadian accent, so the different language spoken by the prince also connected to my reality. It was frightening to leave everything I knew in the United States and immigrate to an unfamiliar place, and also to imagine living on so little income. For good reason, my parents had misgivings about the marriage. This also matched my story.

This decision didn't lead to a lifelong love, but it did result in two beautiful daughters born after high-risk pregnancies. I would never have been able to afford to get the care I needed in the United States. But being in Canada, I was covered by public health insurance, so my pregnancies cost me nothing. I also had access at the local hospital to a specialist who happened to be known internationally for his expertise in helping women who had my problem. He got me through the pregnancies and then passed away exactly three months after the delivery.

Prince Theodore ended up becoming wealthy and both my daughters will benefit from that financial security throughout their lives. I would never have moved to Canada unless it was for marriage, but because I did, I ended up meeting my present husband, who I can say is my true soul mate in every way. I cannot regret one step of the journey that helped me connect with Theodore, because all of it needed to happen in that exact order for my present life with Lee to come about. Maybe I am more tuned in with my destiny than most people. When I met Theodore back in 1988 on a random crosswalk in Minneapolis, I recognized him as someone I felt I already knew. The minute he spoke to me, I knew. His previous fiancé was also named Sarah, which is my name as well. It was clear after that evening that the meeting between us was more than luck; it was meant to be.

A fortune-teller once told me that when two people are meant to be together, God will bring them together no matter how physically far they have to travel. Sometimes, she said, it is also necessary to marry the wrong partner in order to set up the right circumstances for meeting one's true soul mate. Did my childhood book come from my own creation, or did it flow from someplace else, a place where all our destinies are known? I will never know; however, I do know that I have two fantastic "miracle" daughters, now grown, and a wonderful, loving partner to grow old with. In fact, we are so compatible and loving that people sometimes think we have just recently met.

My own will and imagination as a child may have started a chain of events, and became an inner script for the events of my adult life. Had I not had the courage and determination to follow that script, I would never have met my husband Lee, who, after seven years, I am falling more in love with more every day. So, although I do admit that my will may have been required to move to another country, the winds of destiny were always at my back. And I am so profoundly glad that they did!

Sara Harrison, MA, B.Ed., is a freelance writer who lives in Kingston, Ontario, Canada.

Destiny Calls!
By Jim M.

Back in 1998 I applied to start my university course training. I spoke to a woman on the phone at the university I wanted to attend several times before the course started. We had several disagreements and I remember thinking to myself, "What a cow!" and "How unreasonable can one person be!" However, it must be said that the person really being unreasonable was myself, probably because I was getting really anxious about maybe not getting on to the course! Anyway, on the day of enrollment I was ushered toward a slim, very attractive blonde lady, who introduced herself. This was the woman I'd had all the arguments with over the phone throughout the summer!!! Within weeks we were dating, and within two or three months she moved in with me! Four years later we were married in Cornwall. That was eight years ago!!

A Destined Friendship
By Donna Higbee

My life got more complicated as I found myself wanting to get involved with a man at work. He was married, but he and his wife hadn't spoken for months. They were staying married for financial reasons only. I tried to tell myself that I didn't need to start caring for a man who brought all kinds of problems to the relationship. The more I tried to put a damper on my feelings for him, the more I really wanted him to leave his wife so we could have a relationship and be together.

One evening I sat at home on my sofa and decided to use mental telepathy to get him to leave his wife. I took up a meditation pose, focused my mind on what I wanted to accomplish, and then began my process. I had learned some time back that I could sometimes influence people's behavior by a certain process that I had taught myself.

It consisted of sitting very still, building up a level of energy in my body through intense concentration, then linking my strong desire or thought to that energy, and together sending them like a shot out through my forehead to the person in question. I could always tell when I was successful because afterward I was exhausted and drained of energy.

This was what I was going to attempt to do that night. As the energy in my body increased in intensity, I was reaching the point where I was ready to link my thought to this energy and send it, when suddenly I was aware of someone standing right in front of me by the sofa. I don't remember if I opened my eyes or saw with my mind's eye, but standing right there was a very tall man in Eastern clothing staring at me. I could feel the power emanating from him. Almost immediately, he telepathically asked me, "Do you really want this man?" referring to my friend at work. Even before my conscious mind could answer a strong "yes," my subconscious or maybe superconscious mind answered him with a "no, I do not."

When I heard myself say this, I was totally shocked. Of course I wanted this man—what was I saying? The guide accepted this answer, bowed his head, and disappeared. I sat there for some time reflecting on the visitation. Gradually I became aware that I had been saved from making a terrible mistake. I was not meant to have this man in my life, yet I believe that I was given a choice. If the deeper part of me had answered "yes" to his question, I have no doubt that my friend would have left his wife and started a relationship with me. I now know that I would have complicated my life with that decision, had my guide not intervened. Armed with this new awareness, I could hardly wait for work the next day to see how I would react to him. I was pleasantly surprised to find that I only saw him, from that point on, as a good friend and not as a potential partner.

Destiny: I Wed It

By Karen Kramer McAfee

I met Jim back in 1988 when I was a receptionist at a law firm. He called the office often, and we chatted between calls quite a bit. I was really drawn to the sound of his voice. I don't know how to explain it, but there was just *something* very special about it.

Jim was invited to the office Christmas Party, and he asked my supervisor to introduce us. When she came and told me that he wanted to meet me, I was reluctant and shy, but she insisted, pulled me to him, and made the introduction. He was tall, with medium brown hair and a full beard. I don't know if it was from embarrassment or excitement, but his cheeks were bright red under his whiskers.

Ugh.

I hate facial hair on a man.

We chatted politely, and I discovered that he was actually about three and a half years younger than me.

Ugh (again).

Why couldn't he be older?

I don't recall much about the rest of the party, except that it was awkward making small talk. He was persistent in asking me out the following week, and we finally decided that we would meet after work for drinks. I invited my girlfriend to "bump into me" there, just to provide moral support and conversation. (Don't even *try* to tell me you've never done that.)

I waited for Jim to show up on Thursday, and just as I thought I was being stood up, a handsome man with a mustache came over to me and said hello. It took me a minute to realize that it was Jim, but when I did—*wham!* Was this the same guy from the Christmas party? When I asked him why he shaved off his beard, he shrugged and told me that a "little voice" had told him to do it. *Hmmm.*

We talked for hours over beers. Renee showed up just as she said she would, although we didn't need any help keeping the conversation flowing. We were immersed in each other. By the end of that cold February evening, I knew that I would marry him. Don't ask me how or why; I just knew.

Three weeks later, in March, and because Jim lived about a half hour away from me, I gave him a dresser drawer in the spare room to store some of his clothes for the weekends and, well, he never actually went back to live at his apartment. We picked out rings in May, and, just a little more than a year after we met, we were wed.

We have talked often about how we met over the last 22 years, and Jim has always said that he felt the same way as I did: that we were destined to meet. The life lessons and spiritual journey we have taken together could not have been the same with anyone else.

Destiny? Absolutely.

But I also say, "Thanks, Gramma."

Karen McAfee is a medical intuitive and student of spiritual evolution and metaphysics. She is an avid gardener and photographer who specializes in portraiture as owner of McAfee Photography in Lawrenceville, Georgia.

The Phone Call That Saved My Life
By Ginger Voight

I'm a big believer in destiny. From the people I've met to the paths I've chosen, I truly believe that our lives benefit from a little divine intervention. In 1980 I was a new student at Eastridge Elementary in Amarillo, Texas. I started this particular class late because my mother, in her infinite wisdom, decided to move to Amarillo just a few weeks into the school year. Needless to say I wasn't especially thrilled to move to a strange new city with a bunch of kids I didn't know right at the start of fifth grade.

All that changed one day when the person who sat in front of me turned around to start a conversation.

"If you were old enough to vote, who would you vote for?"

Turns out both this other person and I were not too keen on either Carter or Reagan, so we decided then and there we were "Independents" who belonged to neither party.

It was an innocent time.

That person's name was Jeff, and his friendship ended up being one of the greatest things that has ever happened to me. God knew what he was doing when He aligned our paths in 1980. Little did I know I would lose my father in December of that year. My mom worked nights, and without my dad life would have been bitterly lonely. One night Jeff called me and we stayed on the phone for at least four hours straight. This would be a precursor of what was to come. Fifth grade seems so long ago now but our friendship is as strong as ever. This has been despite the fact that I've only lived in the same town as he has for 10 of our 30 years.

My mother liked to move around a lot, and when she decided to leave Amarillo to return to my hometown in 1982, I was crestfallen. No longer could I call just call Jeff on the phone whenever I wanted or needed to talk.

Instead we promised to write each other. Within a week I went out to the mailbox to find an envelope in the mix that was addressed to me. It was on Muppet stationary, as we both shared the love of all

Fig 9B

Ginger and Jeff as teens.

things Beaker. Those letters became the reason I would race for the door whenever I heard the mailman. Though we couldn't call each other, we were still connected.

Jeff was the one I'd confide all my secrets to, and he'd ultimately be the first person I'd tell that I was raped at age 4. That had been my dirty little secret up until I was 14, when a friend of mine was going through a similar crisis, and I was scared and confused and dealing with trauma that never seemed to stay hidden no matter how much I tried to bury it.

On that particular day in 1984 I was so overwhelmed I considered the unthinkable. I sat at my dining room table with a knife quite literally to my wrist in a state of despair I have thankfully rarely known. The moment the steel blade touched my skin the phone rang. I decided to answer it and heard Jeff's cheery voice on the other end.

The thing that makes this all the more miraculous was that Jeff's mom never let him call me. These were the days before cell phones, where steep long-distance charges could stand between two friends who loved to spend hours on the phone. That's why we had letters.

Just hearing his voice made me burst into tears. I told him what was going on and that's when he shocked me by crying himself, telling me how much I meant to him and that I couldn't go anywhere. I didn't know it then, but he was going through his own silent hell, discovering who he was·and who he was expected to be. He needed me, I needed him; the knife was forgotten.

This one event will forever prove to me that there is a God. There is a higher power out there who is quite capable of miracles—and Jeff's calling me that day when I needed him the most is proof positive of that.

This is why when he came out to me years later, I would not forsake him because of religion. I already knew that he was in my life for a reason and I his. I can't question that brought us together— and I thank God daily for the gift.

Ginger Voight is a freelance writer, author of the novel Dirty Little Secrets, *and optioned screenwriter who has been featured in the* New York Times *best-seller* Not Quite What I Was Planning. *She blogs regularly at* www.facebook.com/l/1b311DOSFxvlnY7FIW1w7VlI_EQ;gingeratlarge.com.

Choosing Your Destiny
By Eric Steven Rankin

As a young child, I never got asked if I believed in such a thing as fate, but I believed in it just the same.

I grew up in a safe suburban neighborhood in Southern California during the 1960s. My dad was a banker, and my mom worked for a local utility company. We lived in an enviable home near a private golf course where my dad played golf every weekend. I had no reason to ever believe that my fate would be any different. In fact, it comforted me to think that I would grow up to be just like my dad—a man who drove nice cars, married a beautiful wife, wore a tie to work, and drank martinis after a few rounds of golf at the club. What's more, my micro vision of the world seemed to match perfectly the macro vision that was being sold to my family in magazines and on TV. My parents looked like the people in the car and cigarette commercials pandering to people like my parents, so everything made perfect sense.

But along the way, maybe it was as early as fourth or fifth grade, I began to sense a rift between my personal reality and everybody else's. I was not an athlete. I was drawn to art, creative writing, and music. While my dad and mom wore catalogue clothes and bought department store goods, I was inspired to make things and play music like the poor Italian kids that lived next door to my babysitter on the other side of town. My parents and their friends were living a dream built on luxury and consumerism, but I could not help but notice that that dream was beginning to unravel a bit at the edges.

I didn't know it then, but on a warm summer day in 1969, the path of my destiny was about to take a serious detour. I was listening to my bright red transistor radio when a song came on that magically seemed to open my eyes, ears, mind, and heart all at the same time. As the music played, a sense of cosmic mystery began to build. Flutes drifted in hauntingly, backed by a primal, driving beat, and then there were those words—words that did not make sense to me but seemed familiar just the same: "When the moon, is in the seventh house, and Jupiter aligns with Mars. Then peace will guide the planet, and love will steer the stars."

I suppose this moment, more than any other in my life, is when my sense of destiny and fate began to blur, and it has been beautifully blurry ever since. I did not (at least as far as I know) choose to be a child of impressionable age when the song "Aquarius" came out. I did not make any overt attempt to veer away from the safe and predictable life that my parents had worked so hard to achieve, but I have been steadily veering off that trajectory for the last 40 years.

So was it my destiny all along to write a novel titled *The Aquarians*, a story that advances the idea that we have finally entered the golden age of love, compassion, and peace that the 5th Dimension sang about all those years ago?

Maybe. But millions of people were born when I was born, and they all heard the same song. They all saw the hippies heading off to Woodstock (which, by the way, was officially billed as an "Aquarian Exposition") and were all left wondering if humanity had indeed turned some kind of corner on its evolutionary path of spirituality and higher consciousness. In that regard, we all shared the same "fate" of being alive when this explosion of awareness took place, so why am I the only person that wrote a novel with this particularly Aquarian slant?

For me, it is far more logical to view fate as a process that combines such factors as physical reality that is, place and time), but also the personal realities of perception, attribute, desire, and action. It could be said that a person born into a family of concert pianists is destined to be one himself or herself, but of course this is not true if that person has never made an attempt to play the piano!

In my novel, the protagonist in the story wonders why he has been chosen to learn about and share an amazing discovery regarding the future of humanity's existence on planet Earth. To that, another character responds that he was not chosen, but rather he had actively and consciously made every choice himself that led to the discovery.

Fig. 9C

Author Marie D. Jones and Eric Rankin with their mutual books about the 11:11 phenomenon and the year 2012, at the beach in Carlsbad, California. They met at a book signing and were destined to be friends.

Your destiny, combined with your past action, has brought you this far. The question is, what are you going to do from here?

Eric Rankin is the author of the novel The Aquarians, *a tale of hope for the future. A native of Southern California, Eric weaves his experiences as a Coast Guard–licensed captain and his numerous encounters swimming with wild dolphins into a lush tale of romance and spiritual discovery. His Website is* www.theaquarianage.com.

Kiss That Frog
By Sally Richards

Two things we can count on—death and taxes. Love? Not so much. So why are we always seeking this Holy Grail as elusive as a Higgs Boson? I'll tell you why. When you finally find true love, it takes your breath away, and your heart aches when it slams the door behind it.

I've met four happy couples in my long life. *Four*. Forty-five years of living and I've only met *four* couples truly in love—and who've been together for more than 20 *happy* years. I examined the couples like some extraordinary paranormal find under glass—and like some mad scientist, I climbed to the rooftop of my meta-phorical castle, lightning striking all around, and shouted, "True love lives!" Yes, it does exist, but did it exist for *me*?

As I pondered that question through life, I would often think back on one sunny day in my youth that stands out so amazingly clear. Blue sky spanned the horizons, and the earth smelled ripe. My friend Brenda and I were picnicking with my mom and dad on the shores of a beautiful lake.

I screamed as a large toad landed near me. Caught up in the moment, I scooped him up gently and brought him to my lips. "Are you my prince?" I asked, giving him a kiss on his warty head. Brenda snickered, "Promise you won't set me up with a friend of his." There was no transfiguration in the toad, but I felt something had shifted—something had begun I had no way of stopping. I set down the toad and wondered what I'd done.

I was with another friend, Patrushka, at my parents' house, and we were chatting on the CB radio in my treehouse. I heard a voice clearly through the crackling static. My breath caught and my in-ternal compass pointed north. "Handsome, what's your handle?" I asked in my sultriest 14-year-old-voice. The voice and his friend came to our emotional rescue for the evening. My 16-year-old guy's smile was sly and shy. We dated on and off in high school and college. We mostly bickered; neither of us had any idea what to do with emotions so deep. Then we parted in opposite directions, and were separated by time and space.

Over those years of driving fast down life's highways, once in a while my mind downshifted and I'd slip back in time where I'd find myself in *His* arms, everything around us disappearing as we consumed each other's hearts in sacrifice for an instance of total saturation of our souls. Yeah, it was *that* good, when it wasn't *that* bad.

As the years rolled by, I was one of the first with a blog. I was part of the digerati in Silicon Valley. When the crash hit, I left to Vegas to do a brick-and-mortar turnaround. One afternoon, I knocked off early and went straight to Red Rock State Park. I hiked back to Calico Canyon, where that particular year there was a creek. I sat on a rock and stuck my feet in the cool water. For a moment I was back kissing the toad. "Where is *my* f*&#ing prince!?" I demanded from deep inside the canyon. The words echoed above and disappeared into the afternoon shadows.

That night, I sat in my home office, the warm desert breeze billowing the curtains. I poured a goblet of top-shelf port and continued writing *Ten Bad Men—The Archetypes of Men You Don't Want to End up With*. The premise was men don't change, and by finding the same emotionally unavailable men over and over and trying to change them into something they're not, we make them bad, and we sabotage our own happiness. I heard a knock on the door. I looked to see who it was and my hand froze on the knob.

"Hey," He said.

"Hey," I barely whispered back. "Want to come in?" I asked slowly, unlocking the door.

He gave me a big, long hug. "I was in town for a trade show, heard you were here."

"I want to show you something, and I don't want you to think I've been writing about you for 17 years," I said, printing out the page I'd been writing. It identified His traits—the archetype of The Creative Guy in my book.

"That used to be me," He said, agreeably enough. "It isn't me now, anyway. I'd be happy to show you." I smiled, although it would mean the whole premise of my book was trashed. Men can change, they just have to do it on their own terms. He said he'd been reading my blog. He said it seemed like I was between men. Bottle of wine and Duraflame Log in the trunk, we headed out to Red Rock campground and talked all night. Camp-slot twenty-seven, the same place he'd propose and present me with a ring three months later.

Fig. 9D

Sally and Jeff's bundle of joy, Sidney.

When people ask me if I believe in Fate, I grin. We've been together nearly eight years, and have a little kid running around. We're now the fifth couple. So does Fate exist? All I have to do is look in our daughter's eyes and I know that answer without any hesitation at all.

Sally Richards is an author, paranormal investigator, wife, and mother—not necessarily in that order.

The Alchemy of Love
By Andrew Brewer

Each child comes in to this life with an "optimal path"—the highest integration of all the various talents and desires one has, all lined up and moving toward an expression of pure and total love. This "optimal path" is based upon his or her genetics and past life "themes." Then we lead whatever lives we lead. The difference is a fairly straightforward mathematical formula: "where we are" minus "what our optimal path should be" equals "our karma." I, somehow, am able to see both those states fairly well. As a result, I am able to understand the wounds one has, whether they occurred first in this life or a previous existence, and help individuals integrate and heal from those wounds.

I have done a lot of work on myself over the years and, I think anyway, am starting to grow into a fairly integrated soul. As a result of that inner work, I was able to "see" my way towards meeting "self" in the form of "other"—what you would call a "soul mate."

Because I, literally, channeled her name—at a time when, based upon our respective paths and history, we were most likely to understand and appreciate the beauty of the other—I feel it safe to say that this "recognition" and "coming together" was a result of work I had done first on myself, literally magnetizing this connection to me at, initially, a soul level and then, afterward, live in 3-D here on the physical plane.

Alicia Kent and I have come together, partly as "soul partners" for each other but, on a different level, as co-creators of a way of seeing our lives that, in my opinion, is fairly unique. Her work with Jin Shi Do, along with my abilities as a clairvoyant and astrologer, serve as complementary modalities.

I have been reluctant, over the years, to step fully in to this "soul place," largely because I did not feel worthy to be there. There was always more to do, more books to read, bigger fish, etc. etc. etc. I don't feel that way anymore. I do believe I have "earned"—based on my own internal thermostats—the right to step in to that space, my divine space, and share that divinity (which is within each of us) in a manner consistent with my "highest self." I have lived one life, in order to learn, now it is time to move in to a new life in order to teach.

All my past successes and failures—and there have been plenty of both—were simply puzzle pieces left along the roadside for me, in some Great Cosmic Game, to scoop up and fit back together. I am there now, not close to there, not pretty much almost there—I am there.

Love is the answer. Because I "woke up" to God's Love for me (after Lehna died I was not in a "loving space" with Divine Law, and it took me a while to forgive God—and myself—for not protecting my darling baby), I also woke up to a love for myself, as a fully integrated conscious soul. Love of self *is* love of God.

It is my journey back to that love that underscores my career. I feel as if my work, truly, is at a higher level. Each year that passes, I grow stronger, see more clearly. But love, especially love for yourself, is the key to unlocking the mysteries of Spirit. There is a way back, a door to love and understanding. I see it, finally, for what it is.

Andrew Brewer, known as "The Rock n Roll Psychic," is nationally televised clairvoyant, astrologer, remote viewer, and specialist in the integration of intuition and business. A former business executive, twice selected for inclusion in Who's Who of Executives and Professionals, Andrew is a professional actor, author of three books, and creator of the "Khar-Ma: Past Lives Divination Deck" and "The Tarot of Hungarian Shadows." For more information, please check out www.rocknrollpsychic.com *or* www.jordan-tek-niche.com.

Living the Dream

By Denise Agnew

I used to think, when I was a kid and when I was a teenager, that things were planned out for me. I didn't really understand how I could make a difference for myself. Whenever I tried to do something that I really wanted to do, I would fail. Miserably. So I stopped trying to succeed. Then I tried creative writing and got a teacher who really believed in me. I did extremely well in her class and she always, always encouraged me and thought I was a great writer. I continued to write books and reams of poetry but never expected anyone to see because I lacked self-confidence.

I started to learn, though, that if fate seemed to drop an opportunity into my lap, I'd better not ignore it. In '83 I had an opportunity to go to Ireland for nine days. I'd always adored Ireland (land of many of my ancestors). I almost didn't go because I was a timid sort back then. My mother said, "Go. You must go. You've always wanted to." I did, and boy, it was a trip. A good one and a bad one in some ways. But it was heaven, too.

During the 80s I realized something was missing in my life. I finally figured out that if I wanted something to "happen" in my life that I really, really wanted to happen I had to *make* it happen. I joined an archaeology group and volunteered at a museum because those were things I always wanted to do. Talk about feeling fulfilled. I was in heaven when I did archaeology and museum work. And I was in heaven when I wrote books. In about '91 my husband said, "You should try to get published." I tried and tried. Finally in '99 a publisher became interested, and I've never looked back. I succeeded at something that I'd always wanted to do, and I'm a full-time novelist. But, I have my days where doubt creeps in. I'd say in the last 10 years, though, I've started to take the attitude that I am 100 percent and totally responsible for myself. No one else and nothing else can be responsible. As a result I've noticed a lot of good things happening to me that I think may not have happened if I'd believed it was all predestined or that someone else was in the wrong for this or that. I'm not perfect and I do backslide and want to scream "This isn't fair" sometimes when something happens that I don't want to happen. But that happens less than it used to, and I'm open to exploring things and learning things always.

On the other hand, I do believe that destiny is possible. When I was a teen my number-one fantasy was to be married to the man of my dreams, living in England or somewhere in Britain, and visiting castles.

When my husband called me one day in '95 to let me know that we were moving to England (not too many Army families get transferred to England like Air Force does), I was over the moon! I'd always wanted to go to Britain, where many of my ancestors came from. When we got to England in fall of '96 and I was sitting in temporary quarters by myself and writing about being in England. I had one of those Maslow Peak Experiences. I felt like I'd come home. It was a weird and beautiful experience.

After we'd traveled around England, Scotland, and Wales over our three years, I had another Peak Experience. I realized that the dream, the fantasy I'd had as a teenager, had actually come true. I was living in England with the man of my dreams and I'd visited castles. It was all true.

Today I'm still living the dream. It isn't perfect, but it is a wonderful dream, and I believe that I'm the one creating it.

Denise A. Agnew's Website is www.deniseagnew.com.

This last, but certainly not least, story is my favorite submitted story, because it is about my own destiny as well, and how often the destinies of two people can come together at just the right moment to create amazing things.

Fate and Destiny: A Skeptic Speaks
By Larry Flaxman

"It is in your moments of decision that your destiny is shaped."
—Anthony Robbins

Fate. Destiny. Providence.

These are heady words often bandied about when one is faced with an outwardly inexplicable event or a seemingly insurmountable task. We often tell ourselves that "it is fated" or that "your destiny is predetermined." As an individual who generally leans more toward self-directed potentiality, I have a hard time believing that one's future direction, course, and path are absolutely predetermined. If it were truly the case, couldn't one simply shun personal responsibility and accountability and still be assured of the same outcome?

Regardless, I have had a personal experience that I cannot attribute to anything but destiny. In late 2007 I came across a book that was to have a profound, lasting impact on my direction and path. I am a voracious reader and, depending upon my interest level, can easily digest five to 10 books a month. My normal modus operandi is to read one and then move on to the next book on my nightstand. Once complete, a book was relegated to the nether regions of my memory banks only to resurface during times of need.

Marie D. Jones's book *PSIence: How New Discoveries in Quantum Physics and New Science May Explain the Existence of Paranormal Phenomena* was different. Something about it "spoke" to me. I really cannot explain it in any other fashion. I finished the entire book in one evening, and then re-read it the next night. I literally could not get it out of my mind. I read it cover-to-cover two or three more times and decided that I had to contact the author.

Contact the author? But why? What would I say? This was wholly unusual, for I had read literally thousands of books throughout the years and never once felt moved to contact the author. In fact, my library consists of nearly two thousand books spanning all genres, and I had never once felt the need or desire to reach out to any other author. In this case though, I felt an overwhelming need to do so.

A quick Google search brought me to Marie's Website, whereupon I sent her a short e-mail telling her how much her book influenced me. This was completely out of character for me, and to this day I cannot explain what triggered my sudden departure from the norm. With our similar beliefs and methodologies, we quickly became friends. Fast-forward three years, and together we have written several best-selling books and a movie screenplay, done hundreds of radio and speaking engagements, and written countless articles for major magazines. Looking beyond our existing projects, as Timbuk3 said in the classic '80s song, "The Future's So Bright, I Gotta Wear Shades."

Fate? Destiny? Providence? I think so.

Larry Flaxman is the co-founder of ParaExplorers with Marie D. Jones and is the president/founder of AR-PAST—the Arkansas Paranormal and Anomalous Studies Team. He is a best-selling author, screenwriter, speaker, and researcher currently working on his fifth book. His Web-sites are www.arpast.org *and* www.paraexplorers.com.

Fig. 9E

Larry and Marie founded ParaExplorers together in 2008.

To show just how destinies can intertwine, along with my work with Larry, I also had a very big meeting of destinies over the last two years with a film producer and director, Bruce Lucas, whom I had met many years ago when he read a script of mine titled *Calling Eridani*. Bruce had loved the script and spent a lot of time generously helping me to make it better and improve the writing—and then I got divorced, I moved, and we lost touch for a few years.

Imagine my surprise one day not too long ago when I just happened to check an online lead newsletter for screenwriters, one I had not checked in more than a year, and saw his name. He was looking for two types of scripts, one of which I had, so I contacted him, and it was as if the years we had been out of touch had never happened.

Our friendship reignited and we decided to become colleagues, and we are now developing together a slate of films including one written by, you guessed it, Larry Flaxman and myself.

Funny how fate works, how destiny unfolds—and yet, it always comes down to the choice to, once you are in the right place, at the right time, open the door that is standing before you.

And walk on in.

Bibliography

Baron-Reid, Colette. *The Map: Finding the Magic and Meaning in the Story of Your Life*. Carlsbad, Calif.: Hay House, 2011.

Brave, Ralph. "Building Better Humans." *Salon.com*, June 27, 2000.

Carter, Chris. *Science and the Near-Death Experience: How Consciousness Survives Death*. Rochester, Vt.: Inner Traditions, 2010.

Cheiro. *The Book of Fate & Fortune: Cheiro's Numerology and Astrology*, 19th printing. New Delhi, India: Orient Paperbacks, 2010.

Cowen, Ron. "Cosmic Rebirth." *ScienceNews.org*, November 26, 2010.

Davies, Paul. *The Goldilocks Engima: Why in the Universe Just Right for Life?* New York: Houghton-Mifflin, 2006.

Dolnick, Barrie. "5 Viewpoints About Soul Mates." *Match.com/Yahoo! News*, November 21, 2011.

Duncan, David Ewing. "Discover Dialogue: Geneticist James Watson." *Discover Magazine*, July 2003.

Eckhardt, Mark. "PBS' 'This Emotional Life:' The Small Self: How Your Identity Constrains You." *Huffington Post*, December 2, 2010.

Haisch, Bernard. *The Purpose-Guided Universe: Believing in Einstein, Darwin and God*. Franklin Lakes, N.J.: New Page Books, 2010.

Hall, Alexandra. "Make Your Own Luck." *Women's Health*, November 2010.

Hebden, Sophie. "The Curious Case of the Quantum Arrow of Time." FQXi Community (Foundational Questions Institute Website), June 6, 2009, *www.fqxi.org*.

Hunter-Elsevier, Maureen. "Bullying, Genetics and Emotions: New Research Shows Links." *Neuroscience News*, July 26, 2010.

Karen, Michelle. *Astrology for Enlightenment*. New York: Atria Books, 2008.

Lanza, Robert. "Does the Past Exist Yet? Evidence Suggests Your Past Isn't Set in Stone." *Huffington Post*, August 18, 2010.

Levine, Amir, and Rachel S.F. Heller. *Attached: The New Science of Adult Attachment and How It Can Help You Find and Keep Love*. New York: J.P. Tarcher, 2012 (scheduled).

Lloyd, Seth. *Programming the Universe: A Quantum Computer Scientist Takes on the Cosmos*. New York: Vintage Books, 2006.

Long, Dr. Jeffery, and Paul Perry. *Evidence of the Afterlife: The Science of Near-Death Experiences*. New York: HarperOne, 2011.

Myss, Caroline. *Sacred Contracts: Awakening Your Divine Potential*. New York: Three Rivers Press, 2003.

Nepo, Mark. *Book of Awakening: Having the Life You Want by Being Present to the Life You Have*. Boston, Mass.: Red Wheel/Weiser, 2000.

Novak, Peter. *The Lost Secret of Death: Our Divided Souls and the Afterlife*. Charlottesville, Va,: Hampton Roads, 2003.

Ohotto, Robert. *Transforming Fate Into Destiny: A New Dialogue With Your Soul*. Carlsbad, Calif.: Hay House, 2008.

Rees, Martin. *Just Six Numbers: The Deep Forces That Shape the Universe*. New York: Basic Books, 2000.

Rehmeyer, Julie. "The Destiny of the Universe." FQXi Community (Foundational Questions Institute Website), July 2, 2010, *www.fqxi.org*

Schwartz, Robert. *Your Soul's Plan: Discovering the Real Meaning of the Life You Planned Before You Were Born*. Berkeley, Calif.: Frog Books, 2009.

Voss, Gretchen. "What's Lurking in Your DNA?" *Women's Health*, October 2010.

Wendler, Ronda. "Human Genome Project Director Warns Against Genetic Tampering, Discrimination." *Texas Medical Center News*, February 1, 2008.

Winfrey, Oprah. "What I Know For Sure." *O, The Oprah Magazine*, November 2010.

Index

About the Author

Marie D. Jones is the best-selling author of *PSIence: How New Discoveries in Quantum Physics and New Science May Explain the Existence of Paranormal Phenomena*. Marie is also the author of *2013: End of Days or a New Beginning—Envisioning the World After the Events of 2012*, which features essays from some of today's leading thinkers and cutting-edge researchers. She coauthored with her father, geophysicist Dr. John Savino, *Supervolcano: The Catastrophic Event That Changed the Course of Human History*. She is also the author of *The Trinity Secret: The Power of Three and the Code of Creation*, *The Deja Vu Enigma: A Journey Through the Anomalies of Mind, Memory and Time*, *11:11—The Time Prompt Phenomenon: The Meaning Behind Mysterious Signs, Sequences and Synchronicities*, and *The Resonance Key: Exploring the Links*

Between Vibration, Consciousness and the Zero Point Grid, with Larry Flaxman, her partner in *ParaExplorers.com*. She worked as a field investigator for MUFON (Mutual UFO Network) in Los Angeles and San Diego in the 1980s and 1990s, and co-founded MUFON North County. She currently serves as Director of Special Projects for ARPAST—The Arkansas Paranormal and Anomalous Studies Team.

Marie began her extensive writing career as a teenager, writing movie and video reviews for a variety of national magazines, as well as short stories, including award-winning science fiction and speculative fiction for small press and literary magazines. She is now a widely published author with hundreds of credits to her name.

Her first non-fiction book, *Looking For God in All the Wrong Places*, was chosen as the "Best Spiritual/Religious Book of 2003" by the popular book review Website *RebeccasReads.com*, and the book made the "Top Ten of 2003" list at *MyShelf.com*. Marie has also coauthored of more than three dozen inspirational books for Publications International/New Seasons, including *100 Most Fascinating People in the Bible, Life Changing Prayers*, and *God's Answers to Tough Questions*, and her essays, articles, and stories have appeared in *Chicken Soup for the Working Woman's Soul, Chicken Soup to Inspire a Woman, If Women Ruled the World, God Allows U-Turns, UFO Magazine, The Book of Thoth, Paranormal Magazine, Light Connection Magazine, Alternate Realities, Unity Magazine, Whole Life Times, Science of Mind Magazine*, and many others.

She has been a staff writer for *Intrepid Magazine* and *TAPS ParaMagazine*, and a regular contributor to *New Dawn Magazine* and *Phenomena*.

Her background also includes more than 15 years in the entertainment industry, as a promotions assistant for Warner Bros. Records, film production assistant, and script reader for a variety of film and cable TV companies. She has also been an optioned screenwriter, and has produced several nationally distributed direct-to-video projects, including an award-winning children's storybook video. She has several feature film and television projects in various stages of development, including the movie *19 Hz* for Bruce Lucas Films.

In her capacity as an author and researcher, Marie has appeared at several major conferences, including CPAK, Through the Veil, ParaCon, and the Queen Mary Ghost Hunting Weekends. She has been interviewed on hundreds of radio talk shows, including Coast To Coast with George Noory, NPR, KPBS Radio, Dreamland, and the Shirley MacLaine Show, and has appeared on television, including the History Channel's *Nostradamus Effect*. She has been featured in dozens of newspapers, magazines, and online publications all over the world and is currently developing projects for film and television. She lives in Southern California, with her son, Max. Her Websites are *www.mariedjones.com* and *www.paraexplorers. com*.